Faith in Diplomacy

In this well-written book containing accounts of many delightful episodes in his diplomatic life, Archie Mackenzie succeeds in combining his working principles with his deeply held beliefs in Moral Re-Armament. He describes the problems he encountered right up to the highest level in his profession and how he succeeded in overcoming them throughout his long service in Whitehall and in our Embassies abroad. I know of no one else who has done this so capably and it makes both enjoyable and impressive reading.

Edward Heath, KG, PC, British Prime Minister 1970-74

Archie Mackenzie is a diplomat with a long memory. His knowledge of the UN goes back to 1945, and I was fortunate enough to have him as head of the economic work of the Mission when I became Ambassador in 1974. A man of deep personal integrity, which showed in his professional activities, he was a diplomat of the highest quality. His story is well worth the telling.

Ivor Richard, PC, QC, British Ambassador to UN 1974-80, Leader of the House of Lords, Labour Government, 1997-98

The distillation from a life-time of creative service by a Western diplomat identifying with all parts of the world.

Rajmohan Gandhi, Indian writer and political figure

Archie Mackenzie's book is about faith, diplomacy, and personal fulfilment. It is a testament of gratitude for a life of purpose and service. Its author's life has been shaped by the way in which he found practical expression for his Christian faith. It was a commitment which did not always sit easily with the Foreign Office. But the book is also a significant historical document, written by a former Ambassador who found new challenges in 'retirement', ranging from reconciliation work in former Yugoslavia to Western relations with the Third World.

R D Kernohan, Scottish writer and broadcaster

Faith in Diplomacy

Archie Mackenzie

A memoir

CAUX BOOKS • GROSVENOR BOOKS

vi

First published 2002

CAUX BOOKS
Rue du Panorama
1824 Caux
Switzerland

ISBN: 2 88037 506 9

GROSVENOR BOOKS
24 Greencoat Place
London SW1P 1RD
UK

ISBN: 1 85239 030 1

Book design: Blair Cummock
Typeset in Sabon 11 pt
Printed by Kelso Graphics, Kelso, Scotland

For Ruth

Contents

Acknowledgments

The contours of this book were first sketched by my friend Bob Kernohan on a piece of paper at a lunch table in the Roxburghe Hotel, Edinburgh, in December 2000. As I look now at the finished product, I am struck by how closely it resembles that original outline. Bob has remained throughout as my senior consultant and I am permanently in his debt.

Ginny Wigan also joined the project at an early stage, skilfully deciphering and typing my handwritten text and then coping amicably with my endless stream of additions and amendments. She subsequently became overall editor of the book, responsible for the fine tuning of the text and saving me from many pitfalls. To her, too, I am deeply grateful.

John Milton famously said that 'a good book is the precious life-blood of a master spirit'. My own discovery in producing this small volume, my first, has been much more mundane. It has been that a book needs an assembly-line just as surely as does an automobile or television set. And I have been touched by the wide range of friends who have joined the assembly-line at different stages. Philip Boobbyer and Andrew Stallybrass actually had the vision of such a book well before I had and before Bob Kernohan started to give it shape, and Andrew later assumed the role of publisher on behalf of Caux Books. Elizabeth and David Locke of Grosvenor Books also contributed their publishing skills, with early assistance from Robert Hastings of Dexter Haven. Blair Cummock, with whose family I have been entwined for 69 years, not only designed the cover, the typography and the photographic layouts (with help on picture research from Peter and Margaret Sisam), but supervised the whole printing operation as well. When we finally reached the proof-reading stage, Wendy Pugh, assisted by Janet Paine, focused their professional eyes on the text and removed many blemishes.

But most continuously on the assembly line has been my wife Ruth. Her constant encouragement, her insights and her patience, even when drafts and redrafts threatened to engulf our entire abode, have made the whole exercise not only possible but enjoyable and, I trust, worthwhile.

To all these people, and to other helpers unnamed, I therefore offer my warmest thanks for lightening my task and improving the product in so many different ways.

December 2001   ARKM

1

Beginnings – a Glasgow Highlander

My thirty-two years in the Diplomatic Service have been thoroughly enjoyable ones and, when asked by the younger generation about choosing a diplomatic career, I invariably give an encouraging response. I have to admit, however, that I have not been a wholly orthodox member of the Service.

I never filled in a Post Preference Form in my whole career, asking for a specific job. I accepted whatever was offered, and have no regrets about the consequences. I have never been a big player in big events. My role rather was at the margins of history but, looking back, I can see that I was sometimes instrumental in accomplishing more than I realised at the time.

I found myself in the Service as a result of a series of events, few of which I could control. The successive steers given to me by my professors at crucial moments in my university career were admittedly influential. But the really decisive factors were different. They were the outbreak of the Second World War and the circumstances which led to my being in the United States rather than in Britain at that time; and the fact that at the age of 18 I launched out on an adventure in faith that was to last a lifetime. Ultimately it was this decision which led me step by step, in ways that I could not have planned in advance, into the diplomatic profession. I met with opposition from time to time, not surprisingly. But I also found repeatedly that, when facing difficulties, an ally would appear or a locked door would open.

In retirement when I now awake in the morning and look across Loch Lomond from our home on the eastern shore, my first thought is very often one of gratitude. Not achievement. Not failure. Not frustration. And certainly not boredom. Just gratitude.

This mood is not induced simply by the unspoiled and unsurpassed beauty of the loch and the islands and western hills beyond, which take on a special luminous quality in the early morning. It is gratitude for a host of things, but specially for the people who have shaped and enriched my life.

*   *   *   *   *

I have long thought that G K Chesterton hit on the most original of openings for his autobiography: 'Bowing down in blind credulity, as is my custom, before mere authority and the tradition of the elders, superstitiously swallowing a story I could not test at the time by experiment of private judgment, I am firmly of the opinion that I was born on the 29th of May 1874 on Camden Hill, Kensington.'

In Chestertonian style, I would say that I believe that I was born in Ruchill, Glasgow, on 22nd October 1915 in a tenement flat at 23 Mayfield Street. The only recorded comment on that event came from the Highland minister who baptised me and said in Gaelic: 'He's a small man with a big head.'

My father's forebears all came of farming stock on the Isle of Arran and, if he had had his way, he would have continued in that tradition, but his father decreed otherwise and he was despatched unwillingly to the High School of Glasgow. He eventually joined the Royal Bank of Scotland and served virtually all his career in branches in the Glasgow area.

My mother – who was a Mackenzie before her marriage although no relative of my father – was a Highlander through and through. She came from Ross-shire in the far north-west of Scotland, from the tiny village of Kishorn. On both sides of my family we could, if we wished, claim to be linked to inhabitants of 10 Downing Street. On my mother's side there was a link with Ramsay MacDonald and on my father's side a link with Harold Macmillan whose ancestors came from Lochranza, the small village on the Isle of Arran where my father grew up. But both links are quite remote and they certainly did not affect my own career.

My mother spoke only Gaelic until she was 12 years old. In fact, she retained such a distinctive Highland accent all her life that complete strangers would often say: 'I know where you come from.' Her father was a seafaring man from the same area who owned his own ship, plying the timber trade between Russia and Scotland. He was known as 'Kenneth, the Captain' and wore a gold ear-ring, perhaps as a traditional cure for blindness which overtook him in the end nonetheless. At that point his wife took on the job of postmistress in the nearby village of Kishorn. The old family home-cum-post-office still stands by the roadside, and my wife and I visited it some years ago. The present owner told us that, when modernising the house, he had been mystified to find old maritime charts of the approaches to Murmansk and Archangel in Russia, and Leith in Scotland, rolled in crevices between the first and second floors. He had passed them to the maritime museum in Aberdeen and there indeed we found them – too torn and dirty to be displayed, but still for me a moving evocation of the past.

Kishorn remained practically unknown to the outside world until the 1970s when the biggest ever concrete platform for oil drilling was constructed in the depths of Loch

Kishorn and floated around the north of Scotland to its appointed position in the North Sea.

My mother moved to Glasgow before the First World War and found employment in an insurance office. She and my father met at a church in the centre of Glasgow that was a popular meeting place for young people then flocking into the booming city from country districts to find work.

My father, like my mother, spoke Gaelic and in later years they resorted to it whenever they wanted to prevent my brother and myself from understanding what they were talking about. To our shame, however, neither of us ever learned it.

Five years after me, my brother Kenneth was born, and I suppose one could say that we were a normal lower-middle-class, God-fearing and undistinguished family of four. There must have been over half a million families like us in Scotland at that time out of a population of 4fi million.

Normal living in Scotland in those days meant no shortages, no luxuries and no surpluses. Neither my brother nor I owned bicycles. I never set foot in England, let alone continental Europe, until I was 18. Our summer holidays were mostly confined to visits to cottages in the countryside or at the seaside within a one-hour train journey from Glasgow. My parents calculated that in this way we could get into the fresh air for at least six weeks every year. My father would have three weeks' holiday and then would take a season ticket to travel by train to his office in Glasgow for the rest of the time. Such holidays were rarely eventful but they were nonetheless enjoyable.

Occasionally we went to the Highlands: for example, to Fort Augustus at the southern end of Loch Ness. I remember one beautiful calm summer evening when I was innocently fishing off the Fort Augustus shore. I was about 14 and my mother insisted that, because of the loch's bad reputation for sudden squalls, I should have an elderly local man with me to row the boat. The loch's surface was like glass. Suddenly, however, at a distance of about 25 yards, I saw a large grey glistening back breaking the water's surface. I suppose I saw at least four feet of it. I naturally got very excited and, from my seat at the back of the boat, shouted: 'What is that?' My elderly companion turned ponderously in the direction in which I was pointing, but was too late to see anything. However, by this time the glass-like water surface was ruffled in one spot and ripples were spreading towards our boat.

'Och, it was probably just a big pike, laddie,' said my unimpressed companion. Only years later did I read that a 'monster' had been sighted in precisely the area in which I had been fishing. I will make no further comment – except to say that I must have seen one of the biggest pike on record.

Football was an endless source of enjoyment for my brother and myself – on the streets as well as on regular pitches, and even inside our house. We grew up in the shadow of Ibrox Stadium, the home ground of Rangers Football Club, the blue half of Glasgow's 'Old Firm', Celtic in green and white being the other half. Admission to ordinary matches for boys cost sixpence. But it was much more common for lads like us to hang around the entrance gates until one spotted a friendly-looking adult, even a complete stranger. The cry then was: 'Give us a lift, mister,' and boys of six to ten would be bodily lifted over the creaking turnstiles while the gate-keeper turned a blind eye. By such minor indulgences did enlightened football clubs build up armies of devoted followers long before 'football academies' were ever heard of.

Inside the ground it was standing-room only on the terraces and we were left to our own devices amidst crowds of 30-40,000 (and for international matches, over

100,000) spectators. It never occurred to us – nor, perhaps more surprisingly, to our parents – that any risks were involved. Despite the passions roused by Rangers-Celtic matches, there was virtually no fear of crowd violence.

I retain many vivid memories of my football heroes of those days but, strangely enough, the most vivid of all is of a moment of tragedy. It was at a Rangers-Celtic match in 1931, watched by 75,000 spectators, when I was 15. The game was proceeding normally, with the usual bursts of excitement and exasperation, when a long ball came from the Rangers half of the field towards the Celtic goal. The Rangers centre-forward and principal goal-scorer, Sammy English, raced for it. Simultaneously the young Celtic goal-keeper, John Thomson, dashed out to reach it before English. They met with sickening force near the edge of the penalty area. There was no question of deliberate foul play. It was the sort of sporting collision that might happen at any time. But this time it was fatal. As Thomson dived for the ball, English's boot struck his head. He lay inert on the ground and it was immediately clear from English's frantic signals to the first-aid men that Thomson was badly hurt. In fact, he died that night in hospital from a badly fractured skull. The game eventually resumed and ended, perhaps appropriately, in a draw. But the one unforgettable picture still in my mind is of the ball, after the clash, slowly rolling onwards towards the Celtic goal-line but a few feet wide of the goal itself.

Football was also the occasion for one of my earliest appearances in print. When I was 14, a Glasgow newspaper ran a competition, inviting its readers to summarise in two hundred words their impressions of one of the major Scottish matches. I did not win the prize for the best entry, but the newspaper was sufficiently impressed with my offering to produce a headline saying that 'the man in the crowd' had found a rival in 'the boy in the crowd' and reprinted my effort. The joke was that I had not even been present at the match. I concocted my summary simply by reading several accounts of the match in different papers and then adding my own insights on the players involved.

Intellectually we were awakened by our school teachers, by boys' adventure magazines and by books borrowed from the public libraries. Television, of course, did not exist and even the wireless had little of interest for growing boys. My mother supplemented our intellectual fare by reading to us in the evenings from well-known books, especially by Scottish authors. And on Sunday nights she would read from religious classics like *The Pilgrim's Progress* by John Bunyan.

Some would doubtless feel that this was a very narrow upbringing. All I can say is that we had no feelings of deprivation and that, looking back, I have no sense of regret. However, as I think of those days, I am struck by the realisation that I am describing a pattern of life that has largely disappeared, even in Scotland. Since the Second World War it has been superseded by a new style of life – more mobile, more colourful, more prosperous, more pleasure-loving and sometimes downright materialistic. One cannot return to past times: but especially when adversity strikes, one often gets sharp reminders that there were some aspects of that earlier life-style – for example, the assumptions about discipline and duty – that are still vital to the survival of civilised society.

By 1933 I had finished my days at Bellahouston Academy and, festooned with school prizes, I was ready to enter Glasgow University when an event occurred which permanently changed the course of my life.

Religion, even of a passive variety, was then part of the background of most Scottish families. My parents were assiduous in their Christian duties. As a family we went to church twice on Sundays, morning and evening. In addition I attended Sunday School and made something of a stir by scoring a maximum 100 per cent in five successive years in the nationwide Bible Exam organised by the United Free Church of Scotland. As a teenager, I also had the good fortune in a Glasgow church to meet Eric Liddell, the Olympic Gold Medallist who had captivated the youth of Scotland by winning the 400 metres race in a world record time in 1924, after giving up his chance of winning the 100 metres race a few days earlier because of his religious conviction about not competing on a Sunday. Liddell, much later celebrated in the film *Chariots of Fire*, became one of my boyhood heroes.

My parents took no part in politics either locally or nationally, apart from voting, and so the outside world rarely impinged on our family life. In my final year at school I recall being taken surreptitiously by a much-admired teacher to a Trotskyite study group in a slum district of Glasgow. A small group of working-class men were expounding the Marxist heaven that would result from victory in the class war, but in terms so theoretical that they failed completely to capture my 18-year-old imagination. I also recall the bundles of German banknotes of astronomical value being sold on the streets for twopence after the Great Inflation, which led to the fall of the Weimar Republic and prepared the way for the ominous appearance of Hitler. And I also remember the newspaper billboards proclaiming the sacking of Nanking as Japanese troops marched through China. But such events in the outside world seemed totally divorced from our little family circle – and also from our religious activities.

Early in 1933 I had become aware that my mother had been attending occasional meetings of something called the Oxford Group, then described as a movement for 'first century Christianity' which had grown out of the work of Dr Frank Buchman, an American Lutheran clergyman, amongst the students of Oxford University immediately after the First World War. At the time this Oxford Group had stirred no interest in me. Then one evening she had returned from the meeting saying that the chief speaker had been a man called Sam Reid. Now Sam Reid happened to be the name of one of the dirt-track champions of Scotland at that time. As the principal dirt-track stadium was situated only a mile from our home, the roar of the machines was a familiar phenomenon twice a week, and I shared in the juvenile worship of my contemporaries for the dirt-track stars.

'Not *the* Sam Reid?' I said.

'Well,' said my mother, 'it's someone who owns a garage in Musselburgh and since he met the Oxford Group he has decided to run it on an honest basis.'

And at that moment, for the first time, my attention was awakened to the Oxford Group, whose message emphasised four absolute moral standards – honesty, purity, unselfishness and love – taken from the Sermon on the Mount, and the need to seek God's will on a daily basis. It occurred to me that if people like Sam Reid were involved, it must be religion with a difference. I discovered that the Oxford Group had been spreading internationally, not by any systematic planning, but by a process of contagion emanating from the lives of people – of every background – whose Christian faith had been revitalised by their contacts with Buchman.

Only much later did I learn of a curious coincidence. The name 'The Oxford Group' had first been applied almost by accident to a group of Buchman's friends in South Africa in 1927 and one of the pioneers of his work there was the Very Rev Dr Ebenezer Macmillan, one of the most popular preachers in Pretoria and a Moderator of the Presbyterian Church of South Africa. Ebenezer Macmillan had been born in a small Scottish village near my mother's own birthplace in Ross-shire and was still remembered in the district as 'the local boy who made good'. It was when my mother first heard about Ebenezer Macmillan's association with Frank Buchman that she had decided in her own mind that the new phenomenon of the Oxford Group 'must be all right'.

Some weeks after hearing about Sam Reid, I returned home one afternoon to find my mother having tea with a friend. This lady suddenly asked if I would like to attend a meeting being organised the following night in one of Glasgow's best hotels to hear the experiences of a group of people in the Oxford Group who had just travelled across Canada. They were landing in Greenock and were spending one night in Glasgow en route to Oxford where their summer conference was about to commence. With the thought of Sam Reid at the back of my mind, and intrigued by the idea of a religious meeting in a hotel ballroom, as well as the transatlantic aura of the occasion, I accepted the invitation.

My mother's friend kindly suggested that her daughter and son-in-law could meet me at the hotel entrance, and they in turn found a seat for me in the crowded ballroom beside another Glasgow University student called Tom Glen. He, I soon discovered, had just graduated with first-class honours in mathematics and was going on to take another degree. He later was to become a popular educator in some of Glasgow's best-known schools.

My memories of that meeting, almost 70 years on, are still surprisingly vivid. I was struck first by the vitality of those who spoke. Clearly they had found a spiritual experience which dominated, and even illumined, their lives. They were not great orators but they had interesting things to say. They were not theoreticians; they were practitioners. They were clearly impressed with the response of the Canadians with whom they had been sharing their experiences. The Canadians cited came from all walks of life, as did the speakers at the Glasgow meeting. It was not difficult to credit the comment of the Canadian Prime Minister who had said that their efforts over the previous year had 'been felt from coast to coast' and had 'made the work of government easier'.

Those who spoke at the meeting were mostly British and Christian in background. The experiences they related obviously involved a revitalisation of their Christian faith, but there was nothing exclusive in what they said, nothing narrowly denominational or hostile to other faiths. It seemed to me to be bedrock religious experience and it was well illustrated by a phrase used by one speaker in his twenties which has remained with me ever since. He spoke of finding 'the freedom of glass-house living'. I knew exactly what he meant.

I detected no theological innovations in what was said, but two other phrases with a biblical resonance caught my attention. One was: 'God has a plan: and you have a part.' The other was: 'When man listens, God speaks.' I was to discover in due course that these two dictums were basic to the Oxford Group's message. I also realised on subsequent reflection that both concepts were recurring themes in both the Old and New Testaments.

When the meeting ended I set off homeward with the university graduate who had been sitting beside me and who lived on the same side of Glasgow. However, when he proposed that we meet again to discuss the significance of the meeting, I proceeded to make excuses.

'Could we meet on Friday?' he said.

'No,' I replied. 'I'm rehearsing a school play on Friday.'

'So could we meet on Saturday?' he asked.

'No. I'm playing cricket on Saturday,' I replied.

'Well, what about Sunday?' he persisted.

And so, feeling vaguely that I was running out of

excuses for not doing something that might in the end be quite important, I agreed.

So we met and walked for nearly three hours over a local golf-course. We talked about many things – about the meeting, about our beliefs, about our respective backgrounds – but what I chiefly remember is the straightforward way Tom Glen told me about the steps he, and his father, had taken in response to the Oxford Group's challenge to live by absolute moral standards and, as best they could, to put right what had been wrong in their lives. In his father's case this had involved an apology for rudeness to a neighbour whose dog had been causing problems in the Glens' garden. The neighbours had stopped talking to each other, but the apology had ended the dispute. It was such a commonplace incident and the solution was so practical that it stayed in my mind.

Our walk on the golf-course ended without any drama or decisions. Holidays intervened and I did not see Tom Glen again until the university opened three months later. However, I read some literature about the Oxford Group and the themes of our conversation lived with me.

Some time during this period, without any further prompting, I decided to take the idea of absolute moral standards seriously, starting with honesty. The upshot was that I sought an opportunity to talk honestly with my parents about certain tawdry things in my life of which they were ignorant. I also offered back to my headmaster prize books which I had won in an exam in which I had cheated. Perhaps because he knew that such behaviour was not unheard of amongst other members of the class, he refused to accept them. And I wrote a letter to the secretary of a local golf club explaining why I was repaying the entrance money for an international golfing event when I had clambered over a fence instead of going through a turnstile. I received a warm acknowledgement from him saying that he wished more people would get in touch with the Oxford Group.

Through such simple steps the concept of 'glass-house living' became real to me, and I decided at the same time to start each day by getting up earlier to seek direction, as well as correction, for my life. I read the Bible: I prayed: and I listened. I used a note-book to jot down thoughts that occurred to me: and I checked them afterwards against the absolute moral standards to be sure of their origin and their motivation.

I recall no high emotions at this period of my life, although I experienced what the psychologists call 'the explosive power of a new affection', and I had a sense that these steps were marking moments. I soon felt that my small barque, with the sail up, was moving perceptibly into more interesting waters. So indubitably the Oxford Group, and Moral Re-Armament which it became, were my own channel to a more living faith, just as other valid channels help other people similarly.

I have long been intrigued by the Old Testament story of the man who was instructed by his boss to go to another country, Mesopotamia, and find a suitable wife for the boss's son. It sounded a hazardous undertaking, to put it mildly, and the servant not surprisingly protested. His boss insisted, however, and so the unnamed man set off in faith. Eventually, by an extraordinary set of circumstances, he felt he had found the right girl and she, having heard his explanation of his mission, just as amazingly accepted the proposal and agreed to return with him. Whereupon, according to the Bible story, and one can well believe it, 'the man bowed down his head and worshipped the Lord': and then he offered this simple comment and explanation: 'I, being in the way, the Lord led me.' (Genesis 24. v27. AV)

I too could frequently make use of these words to account for what followed in the years ahead from my first simple experiments in faith.

2

Universities
– Glasgow, Oxford, and the New World

In 1933 I entered Glasgow University with the intention of specialising in English Literature. I had done well in English at school and I knew that I would have to get a job as soon as I could to relieve the financial strain on my parents; English Literature seemed to open the door to two practical possibilities – teaching and journalism.

At the end of my first academic year, however, an unforeseen complication arose. I had done unexpectedly well in Moral Philosophy, coming out top of a class of over a hundred. Moral Philosophy has long been a very prestigious subject in Glasgow University. Adam Smith, the world famous economist, had been professor of Moral Philosophy in Glasgow in the 18th century and his 20th century successor, Professor Archie Bowman, recommended that I should consider switching from the English Literature Department to the Philosophy Department. I was already an admirer of Bowman's, but this proposal came as a complete surprise and presented me with two problems. To make such a switch in mid-course meant that I would have to work extra hard to catch up on the philosophy courses I had missed through specialising in English Literature. And secondly, I had to ask myself: what jobs were likely to be available for a philosopher?

It was in this dilemma that I felt gratitude for the new basis of living on which I had launched in the previous year, consciously seeking God's will in each new choice that I faced. I naturally consulted with family and friends, but I knew the decision must be mine and the inner conviction steadily grew that I should take the risk and switch courses. My parents supported my decision.

My new spiritual experiment had continued undramatically thus far and on reaching the University I had been intrigued to discover that quite a number of students had recently been discovering the existence of the Oxford Group. This led to natural links of friendship – some of which have lasted a lifetime – and with the encouragement of the University chaplain, the Rev Archie Craig, who was later to be the Church of Scotland's Moderator and a leader in the ecumenical movement world-wide. We formed the habit of meeting in his room at 8.30 each morning for twenty minutes to exchange thoughts and make plans. It was not long before a ripple of interest began to spread through the student body, with the normal range of reactions from scoffing and opposition to real spiritual hunger.

Our lives as students at that time were lived against the background of the economic depression of the Thirties that had engulfed Britain. Although it did not affect us directly, it was not long before questions arose in the minds of our small group as to whether our inner beliefs that 'God had a plan for every man' had relevance also to the millions of unemployed and particularly to those in the Clyde shipyards, some of which we could see from the university campus. But how to bridge the gulf between students and workers? One friend then suggested: 'Well, if you want to meet the shipyard workers, come to my church hall. We have given it over to the unemployed to play badminton.'

What began with badminton matches gradually blossomed into wide-ranging discussions on life and work and social solidarity. We were then given the use of an empty hall on the dockside in Greenock, called The Sailor's Rest, where we held weekend meetings composed of unemployed workers and students, and we slept on straw palliasses on the floor. As in the university, so in the shipyards, a ripple of new life and hope became noticeable. Trade union leaders and the management of the shipyards became interested and a culture of teamwork began to challenge the inherited doctrine of class war. This movement continued into the war years and beyond and stimulated international repercussions. Moreover, the links between our group of Glasgow students and the unemployed shipyard workers who responded to the ideas we were advocating survived and grew over the years. Today, over sixty years later, I still count many of these men, now scattered around the world, among my closest friends.

In my third and fourth years I had to concentrate on my philosophical studies in order to catch up on what I had missed by my 'switch'. Toward the end of the third year there occurred an event which seemed a severe blow at the time, the premature death of Professor Bowman, a man of both faith and learning whom I had greatly admired and who had set my feet on the philosophical path. However, he was succeeded by a young unknown Oxford don called Oliver Franks, who was to gain fame as a top governmental official during and after the war, and who, as first Sir Oliver and then Lord Franks, was to become British Ambassador to the United States and was also to influence my own career at a later stage.

My other chief tutor was Professor H J Paton, Professor of Logic, and an eminent Kantian scholar. To him I owe a life-long interest in and affinity with the philosophy of Immanuel Kant. I seemed to respond intuitively to both his

ethical and his epistemological thinking. I liked his empha-
sis on the Categorical Imperative and his non-calculating
theory of ethics, so different from the egocentric views of
John Hobbes on one hand and the calculating style of the
Utilitarians on the other. Similarly on the theory of knowledge I was attracted by the modesty implicit in Kant's
approach. His explanations of the limitations inherent in
different types of human knowledge, contrasting with the
arrogant claims and demands of many rationalists, seemed
to me convincing and left room for realities perceived
beyond the confines of human intelligence.

Looking back, I realise gratefully how much I owe to
the guidance and stimulus of my Glasgow professors. But
I also remained conscious that I was nearing the conclusion of my studies without any clarity on what to do next.
It was at that moment that the unexpected again occurred.
Professor Paton, out of the blue, suggested that I should
think seriously about going on to take another degree, this
time at Oxford. When I commented that this was out of
the question for financial reasons, he replied that he had
been looking into that and, provided my final exam results
were satisfactory, he could assure me that the necessary
scholarship funds could be made available at The Queen's
College.

This was a glittering possibility that had never even
entered my head and it seemed all the more attractive as
the Provost of Queen's College, Canon B H Streeter, a the-
ologian and philosopher, had not long before made a bold
and dramatic affirmation of faith in the work of the
Oxford Group and its founder Dr Frank Buchman. In a
statement that stunned many in senior Oxford, Streeter
said in Oxford Town Hall in 1934: 'I have been watching
this movement more particularly during the last two and a
half years. Hitherto my attitude towards it has been what
diplomatists call "benevolent neutrality" ..... I have come

to the conclusion that in this age of growing world despair it is my duty to associate myself with it.' The conclusions of so eminent a man about the movement with which I was becoming increasingly associated were a source of much encouragement to me.

I duly cleared the final exam hurdles, getting first class honours in Mental Philosophy, when an unexpected and tragic development occurred. When I went out to buy the morning paper, I found on the front page the news that B H Streeter and his wife had been killed in an aircrash in the Alps. This tragedy seemed to call into question the very foundation of my hopes and plans about Oxford. Truly I felt, in Burns's words:

'The best laid schemes o' mice an' men
 Gang aft a-gley.'

All my plans to travel south were complete and in my quandary I felt I could only turn in silence for direction from a higher source.

I still remember the one clear thought that came to me: 'Go: but go to give.' There may seem to be nothing earth-shattering about that: but it was very important to me at that juncture. In a flash it exposed to me how self-centred my motivation still was. 'What was best for me' was still my goal. I suddenly began to realise how important it was to think also about what I might contribute in life and how my own moves might fit into a much bigger plan.

That inner shift of aim and outlook meant that I went to Oxford in a quite different frame of mind and had two of the richest years of my life. Although I did not realise it then, it was also a moral preparation for the next unex-pected crisis I would find myself facing in two years' time.

Oxford was my first experience of living away from home. It was an invaluable experience in every way. It meant not only the full range of Modern Greats (philoso-phy, politics and economics) but an expanding circle of friendships and contacts with a wider and more sophisticated world. It also led to my first personal meeting with Frank Buchman, over lunch in the room of a Muslim student in my college. My initial impression was of someone extremely vital, bursting with energy, a warm personality with an infectious laugh. He also had a pointed inquisitive nose and a strong American accent.

My generation at Oxford (1937-39) lived out its student days against a background of international turbulence and growing war clouds. The Spanish Civil War split the student body and provoked street demonstrations. Appeasement was in the air, but the menace of Nazism and Fascism was growing almost by the month. In my own college, indeed on my own staircase, was one of the younger leaders of Sir Oswald Mosley's British Union of Fascists. At the same time, as we now know, Soviet Communist agents were busy recruiting some of our brightest contemporaries in Cambridge University.

Operating in such a charged atmosphere, we in 'the Oxford Group', ie those in the university who had been touched by Frank Buchman's campaign, took our newfound faith quite seriously. We were a motley group, belonging to many different colleges and coming from a wide range of social backgrounds, as well as from different countries. We used to go down to East London at weekends to assist in the work Buchman and his colleagues were doing there amongst the unemployed – just as the Glasgow students set out to get to know the unemployed shipyard workers on Clydeside. Some of our number were killed in the war that was to break out two years later: many others went on to make their mark in different professions after the war.

We sensed in 1937, even without being told, that if our faith was to be relevant, it had to have a hold on us comparable to the hold that the rival ideologies of Fascism and

Marxism were having on many of our contemporaries. It could not just be a faith for Sundays. In fact we used to gather daily for at least half an hour immediately after lunch, in the library of St Mary's, the university church, to exchange experiences and plan initiatives. We felt we needed to be fit in an all-round way. We therefore accepted the individual discipline of an early morning time of spiritual reflection in our rooms. Indeed, a Canadian Rhodes Scholar used to cycle over to my rooms at Queen's at 7.30 am to share convictions – and, I suspect, to make sure that I was up and doing! He and I have remained close friends ever since and in 2000 AD he won the over-85s World Tennis Championship in South Africa – still obviously committed to the goal of all-round fitness!

In June 1938, responding to the darkening international scene, Frank Buchman made a speech in London calling for 'moral and spiritual re-armament' as the most urgent need of the day. Letters to *The Times* from leaders in politics and the Church showed that he had struck a chord in the national conscience. In August 1938 he held an international conference at Interlaken, Switzerland, on the stark but prophetic theme of 'Guidance or Guns'. In September he addressed a special lunch for League of Nations delegates in Geneva, attended by representatives of 53 countries.

In the ensuing months, as the war-clouds gathered, he redoubled his efforts to awaken the world's conscience to the dangers ahead. He worked mainly from London, but in June 1939 he carried the call for Moral Re-Armament across the Atlantic with mass rallies at Madison Square Garden in New York, Constitution Hall in Washington, and the Hollywood Bowl in California. President Roosevelt sent a message of support to the opening meeting in New York by the hand of the Senator for Missouri, Harry S Truman.

Thus by 1939 it had become clear that Buchman's work, in content and in scale, had outlived its description as the Oxford Group and it became known thereafter as Moral Re-Armament. It retained its direct challenge to the individual conscience but it also addressed itself forthrightly to the world situation. As Buchman himself pungently summarised the development later: 'MRA stands for the full dimension of change – economic change, social change, national change, international change. All based on personal change.'

I meanwhile was pursuing my studies with the help of the best brains available in Oxford, but I was increasingly conscious that I was coming to the end of another phase of my educational career without seeing clearly what lay ahead. I consulted various senior people and it was in early 1939 that Sir Hector Hetherington, Principal of Glasgow University, suggested unexpectedly that I ought to put in an application for a Commonwealth Fellowship under the Harkness Foundation. About twenty of these scholarships were awarded each year to graduates of British universities to enable them to go to the United States for two years to pursue post-graduate work. The money came from the generous endowment of Edward Stephen Harkness, the American industrial tycoon, whose enlightened aim was to enable potential future leaders in Britain to study and learn about the American way of life, as the Rhodes Scholarships did in the reverse direction.

I therefore decided to put in an application and, having survived the early stages of the selection process, I was invited to say what I would study if successful. It was at this point that an unexpected thought came to me in my time of morning reflection: 'Tell them you would like to study "the ethical implications of democracy with special reference to the work of Moral Re-Armament".'

As I was confident that the other applicants would be

offering more orthodox themes for research in science, literature or history, this seemed like a long shot. However, I followed the thought that I had had and was eventually called to London with other candidates to be examined by a selection board consisting of eminent leaders from a cross-section of British universities. I still believe that it was my good fortune that this panel of about a dozen included three Scots – the Principals of Glasgow and St Andrews Universities and the Warden of All Souls' College, Oxford. Anyhow, to my surprise and delight, I was eventually informed in June 1939 that I had been selected as one of the Fellows, and that I should start my fellowship in the University of Chicago in September.

The pre-war summer of 1939 was, however, a time of confusion and alarm for everyone, and so I once more found myself in a quandary. I had the tickets in my pocket to sail from Liverpool at the beginning of September. But what was it right to do, with the shadows of war growing by the day? I agonised about this as the summer went on and consulted as widely as I could on the right course to follow. I found that my three Scottish 'sponsors' on the Harkness Selection Committee (Sir Hector Hetherington, Sir James Irvine and Dr William Adams, CH) all felt that, with such total uncertainty prevailing as to the future, I should proceed as planned.

I duly arrived in Chicago in mid-September and unpacked my bags in the exciting but strange New World. I had followed my sense of what was right as faithfully as I could, but I naturally felt unsettled about how things were going to turn out. In this atmosphere it was not easy to settle down to philosophical pursuits, and I spent most of my time studying American history and culture and following the ongoing efforts of Frank Buchman and MRA to wake up America to the dangers the whole world faced and to provide the democracies with a moral and spiritual infrastructure necessary for the war efforts. In calmer circumstances I would probably have concentrated on my special philosophical research, although there was no obligation under the Fellowship rules to enrol for a university degree. Probably the most celebrated Commonwealth Fellow was Alistair Cooke, the internationally known BBC broadcaster and author, who had completed his fellowship a few years before me, and who had used his time not just academically but ubiquitously to provide himself with the unrivalled knowledge of American ways which has enabled him to go on enlightening a transatlantic public for nearly 60 years.

In Chicago I was immediately introduced into the excitements of American college football, but in the first match I attended Chicago University were defeated by Michigan by 85-0 and the University authorities wisely decided to give up any footballing pretensions. What no one knew, however, was that part of the grandstand of the football stadium was then transformed into a laboratory where the Italian physicist Enrico Fermi conducted some of the experiments in nuclear chain reactions, leading directly to the discovery of the atomic bomb. Although ultra-secret then, a dramatic piece of sculpture by Henry Moore today marks the spot.

Among the enlightened provisions of the Harkness Fellowships was a prescribed tour of the United States during the summer vacation. Despite the prevailing uncertainties, this enabled me to tour America from coast to coast. Travelling by train and bus I was able not only to see many of the scenic marvels of the country, but also to participate in the two political conventions (in Philadelphia and Chicago) where the candidates for the presidential election of 1940 were chosen. In Philadelphia an outsider, Wendell Willkie, overturned the Republican Party machine amidst dramatic scenes and was elected as their presidential candidate. In Chicago Franklin D Roosevelt was acclaimed as the Democratic Party candidate for a third term. Participation, even as a rank outsider, in these stirring events – with all their razzmatazz, music, balloons, parades and speeches – was an unforgettable experience; but it was also a valuable initiation for me into the riddles of American politics, especially in the light of what I was going to find myself doing not long after.

But seen in a longer perspective, the most significant experiences of my transcontinental tour were the weeks I spent at Lake Tahoe in Nevada with Frank Buchman and his closest associates.

The spectacular American launching of Moral Re-Armament at Madison Square Garden in New York and in Washington and Hollywood in May to June 1939 was Buchman's major effort to awaken his fellow-countrymen to the deeper implications of the war-clouds that were gathering. But despite all the efforts of the statesmen of the day, by September 1939 the Second World War had broken out. Buchman therefore felt the need to consolidate his work in the changed international situation and for this purpose gathered over one hundred of his senior co-workers, mainly American and British, for an unhurried time of reflection and reorientation. He obtained simple premises on the shores of Lake Tahoe, then a quiet spot in beautiful country on the borders of California and Nevada. The accommodation consisted of a large chalet surrounded by cottages. The younger members of the party slept in dormitories and all the cooking and all the chores were carried out by the participants in the gathering, which continued for a full three months.

It was there that I joined them in August 1940 for about three weeks. It was an intensely creative time as we shaped the message and the strategy needed in America at that time. I myself, for example, worked on the early drafts of a booklet spelling out for the ordinary citizen the ABCs of 'total defence' of the democratic way of life. Later the pamphlet was distributed in millions of copies across the US under the title *You Can Defend America*, with a fore-word by General John J Pershing, a revered American father-figure who had commanded US troops in Europe in the First World War. Others produced the first versions of musical revues and dramatic productions which were used all over the USA for morale-building purposes during the war years. But most of all, the gathering at Lake Tahoe welded together in unbreakable unity the men and women who provided the international leadership of MRA for the next 20 years.

For me personally those weeks were also a time of importance in deepening my own moral and spiritual commitment, and of course were also directly relevant to the subject of study which I had chosen for my Fellowship. It was a time of profound heart-searching and soul-search-ing, but also of brain-stretching as we faced, personally and collectively, the deepest implications of the war and the threat to freedom world-wide.

Although I had already met Buchman briefly in Oxford, it was at Lake Tahoe that I got to know him properly. He was not an abstract thinker. He was very much people-centred. Part of his gift was to take ancient truths and rearticulate them in arresting ways for contemporary soci-ety. Although the term had not been invented in his day, he was a master of the 'sound bite'. And it is interesting to observe, 40 years after his death, how much of his vocab-ulary and how many of his techniques have been taken over by other Christian communities. It is common today to define the Christian message in terms of 'change', 'God's plan', 'quiet times', 'guidance', 'sharing' and 'life-changing'.

Buchman's critics often accused him of being a snob

who revelled in citing 'big names' as his supporters. But I recollect him in later years devoting as much care and attention to a sweeper and his family in an Indian hotel as to the local maharajah. At one time he was also savagely attacked for being 'pro-Hitler', although in fact the two men never met. But he did reach out to extremists on both left and right in the conviction that anyone could change and should be given the chance to change. Often these efforts were unproductive, including efforts to reach some of the Nazi leaders in the mid-Thirties: but his moral challenge to such individuals was no different from his challenge to prominent members of the Establishment in Western countries.

More remarkable to my mind, and a surer test of Buchman's qualities, was the extraordinary range of people from all backgrounds who became and remained his friends. If I reflect only on friends of Buchman who became friends of my own, and of whom I can therefore speak with assurance, I am struck by their variety and quality. Many of these names will appear in the pages of this book and I shall therefore refrain from citing them here; but there are others in this category that I should at least mention, stretching far beyond my normal diplomatic contacts: industrialists like Frits Philips of Holland, and Yoshitero Sumitomo of Japan; trade union leaders from a score of countries, meeting many of them for the first time through my friend Bill Jaeger, an Englishman whose life work with MRA focused on labour movements world-wide. Then there are sporting personalities like Bunny Austin, the tennis star, Conrad Hunte, the famous West Indian cricketer, George Daneel, Springbok rugby player and pioneer of a multiracial South Africa, and Dickie Dodds, the stirring Essex batsman. There are also ex-King Michael of Romania and his wife; exceptional public servants like Johnny von Herwarth, architect of

West Germany's post-war foreign policy, Allan Griffith, prime ministerial adviser in Australia, and Rajmohan Gandhi, also a prime ministerial adviser and distinguished writer; politicians far and near like Kim Beazley senior, former cabinet minister in Australia; and outstanding women like Mrs John Henry Hammond of the Vanderbilt clan in New York, and Madame Yukika Sohma, life-long social reformer in Japan. Buchman held his personal links with these people over many years, often in the face of attempts by outsiders to sever them, and he did it not by flattery or by bestowing material gifts but by the sheer quality of his friendship and integrity. I know too, as I have said at the beginning of this book, how much such people have enriched my own life.

Buchman was an enemy of the second-best and of the sloppy. He was strict even about the right way to put stamps on envelopes. His zeal may have led him into what some thought were harsh judgements of people: and some doubtless were hurt: but he was always ready to welcome back the prodigal son – or daughter. He could be autocratic but he never claimed to be infallible or 'without sin'. He stood for absolute moral standards and he applied them first to himself and his closest associates. One of his younger helpers said that 'life around Buchman was a mixture of Christmas Day and Judgement Day'. He was exceedingly generous in his use of what money came to him personally and he was moved by a quite unshakeable devotion to the belief that 'where God guides, He provides'.

*   *   *   *   *

In 1940 I transferred from the University of Chicago to Harvard University, still pursuing my basic aim but also still very uncertain about what the future had in store. It was while I was in Harvard that, through a friend working for the British Government in New York, I was made aware that the Embassy in Washington were on the lookout for extra staff, especially with knowledge of American affairs. And so, at short notice and without any prior planning, I was offered a post to make use of the very knowledge I had been acquiring under my Fellowship.

The British Government at that stage were painfully aware that, alone in Europe and even counting on the help of the Commonwealth from overseas, it was far from certain what the outcome of the war with Hitler could be. Everything seemed to hang on American attitudes and help. Despite President Roosevelt's leadership, America was still officially neutral and uncommitted. Thus London was vitally interested in every twist of American opinion. A unit had therefore been assembled in New York, of which I became a member, working under the direction of the Embassy in Washington, to provide London with almost hourly information of the American scene – the campaign of the 'America Firsters', battles in Congress, the activities of the large groups of German-born Americans, the effects of the U-boat campaign in the Atlantic, the unpredictable machinations of the American Communist Party, even after Russia entered the war, the activities of the Zionists, Irish-Americans and other anti-British groups, and so on. It was intensive two-way work: to make London aware of relevant developments as quickly as possible and to help London disseminate corrective information inside the USA. New York was clearly the correct place to contact and influence the American media, but it was not long before it was decided that our intelligence-gathering unit under its distinguished head, Isaiah Berlin, should really be functioning in Washington as an integral part of the Embassy.

Thus by a wholly unpredictable route I became a temporary diplomat in Washington. I felt grateful to find myself employed in interesting and not unimportant war work, but very conscious of how fortunate I was that my footsteps had been led along such smooth paths when most of my contemporaries were in uniform whether they liked it or not. Because of the nature of our intelligence-gathering work, the ebb and flow of the war was constantly before us, but periodically it would also impinge directly and painfully on our personal lives. There were regular visits from close friends like Admiral Sir Edward Cochrane, and my Australian Rhodes Scholar friend Michael Thwaites, already a poet of note, who were both engaged in convoy work as the crucial Battle of the Atlantic see-sawed back and forth. Later there came heart-rending news that my closest friend at Oxford, Ted Hall from Nottingham, had been killed on the Normandy beaches, and a hardly less shattering visit to Washington by my oldest school-days friend from Glasgow, John Marr, so battered from his experiences in the siege of Malta that he was to die prematurely in the 1950s.

Against the background of such events, thoughts about following a diplomatic career after the war would have been not only irrelevant but uncivilised. Yet looking back across the years, I can only feel humbly and gratefully that Providence was at work. There is still truth in Shakespeare's dictum that 'there's a divinity that shapes our ends, rough-hew them how we will'.

3

Wartime Washington – working for Churchill with Isaiah Berlin

The British Embassy in wartime Washington was a vast operation. It also included a collection of specialist missions scattered around downtown Washington – Food Mission, Shipping Mission, Supplies Mission, etc – which were proof of the extent to which we depended on our American ally, especially after Pearl Harbor.

The Embassy itself – in the handsome Lutyens building on Massachusetts Avenue – was more like a sub-Foreign Office. It was full not only of Foreign Service personnel but of temporary staff like myself, many of whom became celebrated in the post-war world in other spheres. I think immediately of Roald Dahl, a dashing Assistant Air Attaché, who became world famous as an author of children's books; David Ogilvy who became almost as widely known as an international mogul of the advertising profession; and David Bowes-Lyon, later of the Reader's Digest, who happened to be a younger brother of the then Queen. Donald Maclean was, of course, also in our midst but I shall refer to his sad case later on.

Outside the Embassy also, Washington in those days was a fascinating crossroad of interesting people. One friendship which I made then in the course of my duties and which lasted a lifetime was with James 'Scotty' Reston

of the *New York Times*. Scotty hailed from the same corner of Scotland as I did. Like countless others, his family
emigrated to America in the early Twenties in search of
better economic prospects. Starting as a junior sports
reporter, he had already graduated into the political field
by the 1940s and went on to become one of the most celebrated and influential correspondents in America. The
Scottish word 'pawky' fitted him like a glove: he was
ingratiating, humorous, shrewd and principled all at the
same time. He probably got as many scoops as any other
political correspondent of his era, but I was never conscious of him deliberately betraying a confidence.

For decades he and his friend Alistair Cooke, *Manchester Guardian* correspondent and BBC contributor from
New York, exerted an influence on British-American relations far wider than any diplomat. We were lucky to have
two such superb interpreters of one side of the Atlantic to
the other; and for both of them the phrase 'special relationship', although sometimes overused in the British-
American context, nevertheless had real meaning.

The Ambassador, Lord Halifax, was a remote but
benign figure. He started his mission in 1941 with several
disadvantages: firstly because of his reputation as a pre-
war appeaser, and secondly because soon after arriving he
misguidedly went hunting, English-style, in Virginia. This
public-relations disaster, especially frowned on in
wartime, was followed by an egg-throwing incident in
Detroit, then a home of isolationism, from which the
Ambassador recovered adroitly by saying how glad he was
to be in a country with enough eggs to throw around. Yet
he ended the war as a much-admired and much-liked figure all over America, and the undoubted turning of the
tide of public opinion in his favour occurred when one of
his sons was killed fighting in North Africa and another
was permanently disabled there. The selfless way in which

Lord Halifax and his wife reacted to this double family tragedy, never allowing it to interfere for a moment with their public duty, made a profound impression on the American people.

My own role in the Embassy was to move in the shadow of my boss, Isaiah Berlin. A distinguished Oxford don, he was squat in stature, ebullient in manner, with kindly amused eyes shining behind thick spectacles. He was decidedly Jewish-looking and had a peculiar gait, slightly affected, which – as I have since often thought – closely resembled that adopted by the actor David Suchet in his brilliant portrayal of Agatha Christie's Belgian detective Hercule Poirot on British television.

Isaiah Berlin was brilliant to the point of genius and in the post-war world acquired an international reputation as one of the sages of the 20th century. But if ever a person was born needing a Man Friday, it was Isaiah, and I suppose I filled that role – at least as regards his official activities – for three exciting years. He broke every rule of social etiquette – regularly forgetting appointments or addresses – and yet he remained one of the top catches of all Washington hostesses. He was a brilliant conversationalist and raconteur; witty but rarely ascerbic; sceptical but not cynical; mischievous yet not malicious; exasperating and yet disarming and possessed of an immense bonhomie. I recall an occasion long after the war when my wife and I were invited to have tea with him in the Garrick Club in London. We emerged two hours later, greatly stimulated intellectually but still without having had sight of a teacup.

The whole story of Isaiah's wartime sojourn in America is a strange one. It begins like a whodunnit and ends like a fairy tale. His arrival in New York was inauspicious. In July 1940 he and Guy Burgess, whom he had known in Britain in the Thirties, arrived together announcing that they were on their way to take up posts in the British Embassy in Moscow, but were travelling via Vladivostok. A few days later Burgess mysteriously departed again for London, leaving Isaiah on his own. Later the British Ambassador in Moscow, Sir Stafford Cripps, let it be known that he felt he had not been properly consulted about these two proposed additions to his staff and the whole scheme was called off.

It is difficult to put together all the pieces of this strange episode and Isaiah did not talk much about it. What is totally certain, to my mind, is that he had absolutely no inkling of Burgess's secret loyalties and subterranean activities as a Soviet agent – as later revealed. And my guess is that he fell in with the Moscow project, which had the approval of senior officials in London, only because of his unhappy state of mind following the declaration of war in 1939. His scholarly world of words and ideas had been eclipsed by a world at war. Where did he fit in? He had no wish to be neutral, given his Jewishness; but it would be difficult to visualise anyone less suited for service in the armed forces. His first offer of his services in a civilian capacity was turned down because of his foreign birth in Riga. On the other hand, the brightest of his Oxford contemporaries were leaving to be co-opted into key positions in the war effort. His morale was therefore low and this was why – as I believe – he became a participant in the abortive Moscow project which was really Burgess's brainchild.

Now Isaiah found himself stranded in New York: stranded but not without friends. In New York he quickly began to make contacts with some of the leaders of the large Jewish community, amongst them Felix Frankfurter, a Justice of the US Supreme Court. In Washington he went to stay with John Foster, an Oxford friend who was now legal adviser to the British Embassy.

His letters show that at first he was not greatly attracted to the style and tempo of American life. He missed the 'nuances' of Europe and Oxford. Yet he quickly acclimatised himself and began to develop an expanding circle of influential friends, both in New York and Washington. Thus it might almost be said that – quite unwittingly – Guy Burgess had rescued Isaiah from the depression that had dogged him during 'the phoney war' and had opened up a glittering new chapter of his life in America.

The Americans for their part seem to have been at once mystified and fascinated by this odd kind of Englishman who spoke at such high velocity and often as if he had a ping-pong ball in his mouth. Yet by his vivacity and acumen, he quickly became a known personality in American East Coast society.

It was on these friendships that Isaiah built up the position of influence which enabled him, later in the war, to become a confidential conduit of information between the British Government and the different sections of the Zionist movement in America – especially with Dr Chaim Weizmann, one of his closest friends. His usefulness to the British cause was thus being demonstrated by his capacity to argue the British case in influential circles, not only Jewish by any means, which were not readily accessible to ordinary British officials. And all this was happening almost before his own Embassy career had begun.

It was in fact through his friendships with John Foster, Jack Wheeler-Bennett and Aubrey Morgan, all then working for the British cause in Washington, that the idea was hatched that a place might be found for him in the Embassy's employ. It was they – not some far-seeing personnel planner at the heart of the war-effort in London – who 'sold' Isaiah to Lord Lothian, Lord Halifax's predecessor. One of his first trial assignments, as recounted in Michael Ignatieff's absorbing biography of Isaiah (*Isaiah*

Berlin, a Life, Chatto & Windus 1998), was to prepare an analysis of the objectivity, or bias, of the Associated Press's reporting of the war in which America was not yet officially involved. And this led directly to Isaiah's employment first in the British Information Services in New York and then in the Embassy as head of the political reporting unit until the end of the war.

Isaiah's forte lay in sniffing out news from all kinds of places, in dissecting and clarifying motives, and in expressing his views in elegant and witty prose. His confidential reports – and especially his weekly Political Summary which went out under the Ambassador's name but was known everywhere to be Isaiah's brainchild – were considered essential reading in Whitehall by everyone from Winston Churchill downwards. Thirty years later, when the conditions of the Official Secrets Act permitted it, the summaries were published in toto in a 617-page volume, edited by Herbert Nicholas of New College, Oxford, who had been their chief 'handler' in Whitehall during the war.

It is now known that the Washington reports were then being enjoyed not only in Whitehall but in Buckingham Palace. Isaiah's fame was spreading and when Mrs Churchill heard in February 1944 that Mr Berlin was in London, she immediately informed the Prime Minister with the hilarious consequences that have been so often retold – and embroidered on, not least by Isaiah himself – of the lunch party at 10 Downing Street when Churchill entertained Irving Berlin, the song writer, under the impression that he was Isaiah Berlin, the political philosopher.

By the end of the war Isaiah had acquired an enormous personal influence on both sides of the Atlantic: but it was influence without power, for he finished the war still holding the modest position of a diplomatic First Secretary. Nevertheless wartime Washington was unquestionably the launching-pad of his illustrious post-war career.

My own role in the Embassy as amanuensis to Isaiah, as newsgatherer, as recorder and editor was absorbing. Although I had not known him in Oxford before the war, we struck up a friendship that lasted a lifetime. After the war our paths diverged and we saw one another only rarely, but I was touched by something he said privately to my wife in the 1980s when I was invited to speak in Oxford about my experiences in the United Nations. Isaiah listened to my story and at the end of the evening said quietly to my wife: 'It is good in life to meet a man who never changes.' I took this as his way of saying how much, although our metaphysical outlooks differed greatly, he respected faith and constancy.

Fifty years later revisionist historians may be decrying Churchill's role in the war, but on a personal basis I can only say that his wartime visits to Washington to see President Roosevelt had a most energising effect on the staff of the British Embassy and always heightened British prestige in Washington and across the United States. Normally we saw very little of him during these high-level and usually fleeting visits, but I recall an occasion in 1943 when it was suggested to him – I suppose by Lord Halifax – that it would be good for morale if he could spare time to meet the Embassy staff. To this the Prime Minister agreed. In response to female pressure, it was then put to him that it would be tactically helpful if wives of Embassy staff could also be invited to the meeting. To this also Churchill agreed: but when it was suggested that the children of the staff might also be included, the great man growled and protested: 'But who do they think I am, a giant panda?'

*   *   *   *   *

When, 50 years on, I recently re-read some of our political summaries from wartime Washington I was struck both by how much we knew, for example, about the minutiae of American politics, and how much we did not know, for example, about the inner motivations of individuals and the ultimate significance of many events. But further reflection produced two deeper realisations: firstly, what immense changes were occurring in America in those five years 1940-45; and secondly, what a complicated task the leadership of the United States, and notably President Roosevelt, had in steering America through this period.

The American scene is so vast and varied that generalisations are always dangerous: there is sure to be an exception or a contradiction round the next corner. Nevertheless, I remain convinced that the transformation that occurred in the American psyche and outlook in this five-year period was one of the major historical developments of the 20th century. When I arrived in 1939, America was still enjoying her sense of isolation from other continents. She had no thought of dominating the world. Her first reaction to the outbreak of world war was to intensify her desire to keep out.

I still recall with emotion an incident that happened to me on a crowded streetcar in Chicago early in 1940. Apropos of nothing at all, unless he subconsciously detected something foreign about me, the ticket-collector suddenly announced to his passengers in a loud voice:

'Why the hell should we help dead-beats who couldn't even pay their war debts?'

My sense of shock was heightened by the fact that the crowded car accepted this outburst without a murmur of dissent as being a perfectly sane and acceptable point of view. I felt cowed and very much alone. I completed my journey without – I admit – making any attempt to challenge the ticket-collector or enlighten my fellow passengers.

The population of Chicago, of course, contained large

numbers of German immigrants, but there were also sub-
stantial contingents from Poland and other European
countries which were already suffering from Hitlerism. Yet
no one on that streetcar wanted to take sides. Their new
lives in America, if they were immigrants, were certainly
not without difficulty, but they manifestly had no desire to
get involved in the latest disasters of the old world.

Another Chicago memory confirms the mixed emotions
prevailing in America at that time. I was taking a normal
car-driving test and was being given a hard time by the
examiner whose voice betrayed clearly his Irish-American
origins. On his instructions, I was having to dodge in and
out between street-cars on a busy thoroughfare when he
suddenly said:

'You'll be from England, are you?'

'Not exactly,' I replied. 'I'm Scottish.'

'Oh, that's different,' the examiner replied. 'I thought
you were a bloody Limey. Here's your licence.'

Gradually, as stories of the horrors of the blitzkrieg
multiplied in the American media, these attitudes were
modified and humanitarian efforts developed in order to
help both Britain and other affected European countries,
but there is no denying the immense task President Roosevelt faced in turning round the American ship of state.
Even proposals to strengthen America's own defences, let
alone proposals to help friendly European countries, got
through Congress only by the slimmest of margins. The
deadly U-boat campaign in the Western Atlantic – some
sinkings took place within sight of the American shore –
did shock many people on the eastern seaboard; but without the Japanese aggression at Pearl Harbor it remains
doubtful in my mind whether President Roosevelt could
ever have succeeded in carrying Congress and the American people behind open and active measures to crush
Hitler.

Yet history turned out very differently. The big change began on 7th December 1941 at Pearl Harbor, and well before 1945 the United States had become the dominant military force contending both in Europe and the Pacific. The news of the first atomic blast in New Mexico symbolised the dramatic turnaround that had taken place. The fact that the conference to set up the new world security organisation took place in California in 1945 and that the United States Senate ratified American membership of the United Nations Charter by a huge majority (89-2) by July 1945 – contrasting so vividly with Congress's depressing rejection of the Versailles proposals for setting up the League of Nations in 1919 – further dramatised what had occurred. A new era had dawned.

Moreover not even the sudden death of President Roosevelt checked the process of change. Harry Truman was regarded as an unknown quantity by most commentators when he was pitchforked into world leadership in April 1945; but, apart from a few initial stumbles, he donned Roosevelt's cloak and, surprisingly, it seemed to fit. Moreover, the American public followed him. Not only did the Senate approve American membership of the UN much more speedily than anyone expected, but American cities began competing against each other with bids to get the new organisation to come and build its headquarters within their walls. And when the appalling post-war weakness of the European countries was laid bare in 1946 and 1947, the United States stepped in to help with what Churchill called 'the most unsordid act in history' – the Marshall Plan.

It was a privilege to be in the British Embassy then tracking these momentous changes. They surprised us as they surprised virtually everyone. In our reports we recorded gratefully the major moves in American opinion that were visible around us, and especially in the outlook of the Republican Party, but we debated seriously how profound they were and how long they would last. How wrong we were.

Later in the 20th century the United States would often get hotly irritated with the United Nations for a wide variety of reasons large and small. At one point in the 1970s an exasperated US official said to a UN body, 'If you feel like that, you can all go down to the docks and sail off into the sunset. We couldn't care less.' But, apart from the geographical impossibility of sailing westward from New York City, there has never been a serious danger of the United States withdrawing from the United Nations. The sea-change that came about in 1940-45 has been permanent.

To the inevitable query as to what brought about such a historic transformation, a number of converging explanations would have to be offered. I would cite five. First, of course, there was the sheer impact of the war itself: Pearl Harbor, the battle casualties, the atomic bomb, the concentration camps, and so on. Secondly, one would have to mention the enlightened American leadership of Roosevelt, Truman, Marshall, Eisenhower, Acheson and many more. They were an exceptionally able band of men. Thirdly, there was the impact of the media. Even without television, the front-line reports by press and radio commentators, like the celebrated Ed Murrow from London and many more, penetrated even the thickest isolationist hides.

Fourthly, there was the phenomenon of Russian ruthlessness. Throughout most of the war, despite America's reputation as the headquarters of capitalism, Soviet Russia had been getting an extremely favourable press in the United States, thanks to her all-out military effort and the heroic defence of Leningrad and Stalingrad. Gradually, however, Stalin's ruthless behaviour was counteracting this positive attitude and sowing doubts about the future. The conflict of opinion came to a head dangerously over Poland as we shall discover in the next chapter; and events in Poland, as we now know, were one of the things that triggered Churchill's private message to President Truman on 8th May that he feared that 'an iron curtain' might be coming down across Europe. However, it was only after Churchill's famous but controversial speech in Fulton, Missouri, in March 1946 that American opinion woke up and the United States took over the leadership of the Western World in facing the dangers of the Cold War that lay ahead.

It is now known that early in the war Sir William Stephenson, the 'Man called Intrepid' who was heading the British Security Organisation in New York, made a report to President Roosevelt who was then concerned about American security even though the United States was not yet involved, in which he said: 'The Nazi programme for the moral disintegration of ideological enemies regards the Americans as the last and largest enemy.'

I would therefore mention, as a fifth factor in bringing about the remarkable transformation of American outlook which I have been describing, the campaign which Frank Buchman had been waging for the moral rearmament of America. I have already referred to the preparations for this campaign which I saw being made at Lake Tahoe, Nevada, in 1940.

While in Washington, I maintained my close association with him in so far as my official duties permitted. This was made easier by the fact that I, as a bachelor, was invited to stay as a paying guest in the home of Jack and Connie Ely on Massachusetts Avenue, not far from the British Embassy. Indeed, their gracious home had once been the Swiss Embassy; but during the war, as well as serving as the Elys' family home, it became an unofficial embassy for the work of MRA, and people from every background passed through its doors.

There is no doubt in my mind that MRA's expanding work all across the United States, and the numerous visits paid by US congressmen to MRA's European centres immediately after the war, contributed to the enlightened mood which prevailed in Washington at that time, leading to such historic post-war initiatives as the Marshall Plan. Indeed, Paul Hoffman, administrator of the Marshall Plan, described Buchman's work as 'the ideological equivalent of the Marshall Plan'.

I remained in Washington till the end of the war, deputising for Isaiah Berlin whenever required and taking over his duties when he returned to Oxford in the summer of 1945. But as the war entered its final phases, I was being drawn more and more into special duties connected with the shaping of the post-war world.

4

San Francisco
– the post-war world takes shape

As early as the spring of 1943 I was temporarily seconded from my Embassy post to act as press
spokesman for Britain at the international food conference
that was convened at Hot Springs, Virginia. I suppose that
my nomination for this job was due to the familiarity with
the American media which I had acquired in my political
intelligence work. Certainly my appointment could not
have been due to my special knowledge of the subject matter that was on the agenda at Hot Springs!

In the event this lack of technical background did not
matter too much because of the unusual constraints on the
job I was required to do. The conference centred in a
stately hotel in the Virginia countryside. But this being
wartime, the American authorities placed a cordon of helmeted troops on duty around the hotel 24 hours a day.
The international press representatives were kept outside
the security perimeter and were allowed inside for only
one formal press conference with the leading delegates. On
that very evening, however, a violent thunderstorm
engulfed the area, all the hotel lights went out and the
press conference ended in chaos.

The food conference did, however, eventually come up
with constructive recommendations and was, in fact, the

progenitor of the Food and Agricultural Organisation which is still a vital part of the UN system, with head-quarters in Rome. To that extent, the Hot Springs confer-ence was significant as one of the first attempts to put in place the building blocks of the post-war world. President Roosevelt went so far as to say that it was 'an epoch-mak-ing demonstration that free peoples all over the world can decide on a common machinery of action'. That may sound slightly over-the-top, but it is true that a pattern was being created of the new multilateral conference diplomacy that was to become characteristic of the post-war world.

Although I contributed very little to the subject-matter of the conference, I did begin to learn a lot about govern-mental publicity methods and about the processes of pol-icy formulation and public presentation.

One year later, in August 1944, I was again seconded from my Embassy duties to act as spokesman for the British delegation at the Dumbarton Oaks Conversations in Washington, where the first drafts of what was to become the United Nations Charter were laboriously ham-mered out. These talks took place in a large mansion on the outskirts of Washington which had already been offered by the Bliss family to Harvard University as a research centre, and which is still in use for that purpose today.

The participants in the Conversations were the top diplomats of the United States, Britain, Soviet Union and China. However, the Conversations were conducted in rather an odd way, because the Soviet Union refused to sit down with the Chinese representatives who were – inevitably at that stage – all members of Chiang Kai-shek's Nationalist Government. So America, Britain and the Soviet Union first discussed the draft papers submitted by each of them and containing their ideas on the shape of a post-war organisation to preserve international peace and security; and then America, Britain and China went over exactly the same ground again once the Soviet Union had withdrawn. The Conversations lasted from August to October 1944.

The Dumbarton Oaks mansion was surrounded by extensive gardens enclosed by a wall and once again, as the war was still on, the US Government decreed – despite howls of protest from their own media – that the conference centre should be protected by helmeted troops. This greatly cramped the efforts of myself and my American, Russian and Chinese colleagues but a system of informal briefings was tacitly permitted in order to keep the world public informed in the most general way about what was going on. Looking back, the obsession with physical security seems rather comical, for *inside* the perimeter roamed a prominent member of the US delegation, Alger Hiss, who was later to be charged in one of America's most dramatic spy trials, the Pumpkin Papers case.

Moreover, even during the Dumbarton Oaks discussions, the elaborate press restrictions became a farce and a matter of great embarrassment to the US Government and its allies because day after day the *New York Times* published *in toto* the main negotiating drafts of the different delegations. These sensational scoops appeared under the by-line of Scotty Reston, their Washington correspondent, to whom I have referred earlier. As Reston had been born and brought up in the West of Scotland and was known to be a good friend of mine, it was almost inevitable that some people would suggest that I was a possible source of the leakages. I am glad to say, however, that my own bosses on the British Delegation and in the Embassy never for an instant betrayed any loss of confidence in me. Forty-seven years later Reston revealed in his memoirs that the documents in fact had been given to him by a young member of the Chinese delegation, who had earlier been a protégé of Iphigène Sulzberger, the wife of the publisher of the *New York Times*.

The Dumbarton Oaks Conversations occurred when the Soviet Union and the Western powers were still wartime allies. The Cold War lay in the future. Therefore an impressive degree of unity was achieved in the talks regarding the shape and powers of what was to be called the United Nations. On one major issue, however, it was impossible to reach any agreement. Andrei Gromyko, the Russian delegate, refused to contemplate any compromise in any circumstance on the Soviet Union's power of veto over all proposals in the Security Council.

The Great Powers' right of veto over important matters was accepted by everyone as a necessity. Put more positively, it was called 'the principle of unanimity amongst the five Permanent Members of the Security Council' – ie the United States, the Soviet Union, Britain, China, plus France. They had borne the burden of the war and it was assumed that they could continue as allies and accept the burden of maintaining peace after the war's end. It was also believed that there would be no chance of getting the US Senate to approve of American membership of the new organisation unless the US Government had such a right. Britain was no less insistent than any of the others on holding a veto power, with our far-flung responsibilities in the Empire and Commonwealth in mind.

Moreover, in defence of their position, it was argued by the Big Five that the new organisation would at least be more democratic than the League of Nations had been. Whereas the Covenant of the League laid down that important decisions had to be taken by unanimity, the draft UN Charter envisaged decisions by a qualified majority – seven out of eleven – provided only that the supporters of important motions included all five permanent members.

The crux of the controversy was how 'important' matters were to be defined, and at Dumbarton Oaks it became clear that the Russians were going to insist that the veto right, or the unanimity principle, should apply to virtually everything, including the control of the agenda and the discussion of the peaceful resolution of disputes where no question of the use of force would arise. Moreover they insisted that a permanent member should retain its power of veto even in cases where that country was itself party to a dispute. It was immediately apparent to the Western countries that such a dictatorial proposal could never be sold to the rest of the democratic world. No organisation would be possible on this basis. However, Gromyko told the British delegate, Sir Alexander Cadogan, that the Russian position was 'final and unalterable'. This was a disquieting revelation of the extent of Moscow's distrust of the rest of the world, a harbinger of troubles to come.

Another attempt to complete the unfinished business of the Dumbarton Oaks Conversations by breaking the impasse over the veto was made at the Yalta conference where Roosevelt, Churchill and Stalin met in February 1945. The priorities and atmosphere there were very different from Dumbarton Oaks where the United Nations was the only subject on the agenda, and the discussions were often rather theoretical and abstract, if not idealistic. At Yalta, on the other hand, the end of the war was in sight and the future of Europe had to be agreed. In such a show-down it was very clear that the future of Eastern Europe mattered a great deal more to Stalin than the details of voting in the UN Security Council.

The controversies at Yalta came to a head over the formation of the future government of Poland. Was it possible to merge the communistic Lublin Poles, supported by the Moscow, with the Polish government-in-exile in London who had worked with the Allies throughout the war?

Averell Harriman in his memoir *Special Envoy* tells vividly how Stalin and Molotov twisted and turned at Yalta to avoid any compromise over their exclusive support for the Lublin Poles. In the end, says Harriman, they 'effectively detoured the conference', which should have been discussing a proposal of Roosevelt's to bring representative Polish leaders from different parties to Yalta immediately to thrash out an agreement on the spot. Instead Molotov pretended that he could not contact the Lublin Poles in time and Stalin then suddenly announced a Russian concession over the voting methods in the Security Council. The concession – to remove the veto from discussions on the peaceful settlement of disputes while retaining it in all questions involving the use of force – was quickly accepted by the Western leaders: but Stalin got his way over Poland, and Poland suffered grievously for 45 years as a result. With the gap in the Dumbarton Oaks proposals filled, the three leaders then also agreed to hold an international conference in San Francisco in April 1945 to finalise the drafting of the Charter of the United Nations.

The San Francisco Conference opened on 25th April 1945 and I was sent out ahead of time to set up the press relations office of the British delegation. It was the most remarkable and enjoyable intergovernmental conference I have ever attended. I believe it came closer to the 'Congress dances' mood of the Vienna Conference of 1815 than any other conference in the 20th century. Everything seemed to contribute to the euphoric mood.

First, there was the Californian sunshine and abundance of food which made a sharp contrast with the European black-outs and ration books familiar to so many of the delegates. Secondly, there was the boundless generosity of the local population and their visible pride in the presence of so many world celebrities in their midst. Thirdly, there was the imminent end of the war in Europe which happened shortly after the conference began (Californians, however, were very conscious of the continuing war in the Pacific as San Francisco was full of departing soldiers and sailors, and all bars were closed on VE Day to prevent inappropriate demonstrations of jubilation – much to the dismay of the European delegates). Finally, there was the fact that many of the diplomats from around the world were meeting their *chers collègues* again for the first time since 1939. Optimism was in the air.

I think it was because of these contributory factors that the conference made such remarkable progress. Indeed, compared with intergovernmental conferences in the ensuing decades, it was amazing how much the conference achieved in a relatively short time. Yet it was not very long before some of the underlying problems in setting up a new international security organisation began to surface and the initial euphoria was punctured. And it was at that point that the two sides of my own involvement – professional and moral – again came together.

While it is a fact that Churchill, Roosevelt and Stalin decided in February 1945 that the UN conference should take place in San Francisco in April, it is also a fact that five months earlier, in October 1944, Frank Buchman at a planning session at MRA's conference centre on Mackinac Island, Michigan, had already decided that a large-scale campaign for moral re-armament should centre in California in the spring of 1945. Call it premonition or call it coincidence, the fact is that when the international diplomatic community arrived in San Francisco in April they found a large force of MRA workers already active in the area. Buchman's campaign was aimed at raising morale in the local community, especially in the defence industries and the docks, and at preparing people intellectually and psychologically for the challenges of the post-war world.

When the UN conference began Buchman made no bid

to attract attention to MRA or to himself. He had no official status. He confined himself at the start to making friendly contact with delegates – and there were many – whom he or his co-workers had known previously; and he established himself most days at a circular lunch table in the Fairmont Hotel. (He was still walking with difficulty following a stroke he had suffered in 1942.) I and some of those in his entourage were then able to bring many of the conference personalities to meet him at his table, either for informal lunches or short conversations. In this way he kept abreast of developments in the conference and expanded his circle of friends among the delegates. This was Track Two diplomacy at work decades before that current term had been invented. In fact the contacts Buchman made at San Francisco provided the springboard for many of MRA's advances around the world in the ensuing decades.

My own professional duties at the conference kept me extremely busy. In contrast to the stringent security regulations that had prevailed at the Hot Springs conference and Dumbarton Oaks, San Francisco was like a goldfish bowl. The centre of operations was – symbolically enough – the city opera house, and the US Government – who were responsible for all practical arrangements – had clearly come to realise that it was necessary to cultivate public interest in the proceedings in preparation for the ratification hearings which would inevitably follow in Washington if the San Francisco conference succeeded in producing an agreed draft charter for the UN organisation. Thousands of newspapermen and photographers therefore swarmed around the conference hotels and meeting centres. The British security authorities were not a little concerned when they discovered that the American columnist Walter Winchell, famous for his eavesdropping, had managed to reserve a suite on one of the same floors in the Mark Hopkins Hotel as their delegation was using. This nervous excitement reached fever pitch when technicians from one of the American radio networks were found wiring up Anthony Eden's hotel bathroom with microphones in the hope of getting a scoop interview at the very instant when the end of the war in Europe was announced.

Gradually, however, as so often happens at such gatherings, the initial press optimism wore off. As the difficulties in the discussions increased, the tone of comment became more sceptical and impatient. Predictions even appeared about a possible need to adjourn the conference without full agreement. Three issues in particular were felt to be endangering the conference. One was Poland, whose future had already become a bone of contention between Roosevelt, Churchill and Stalin at the Yalta Conference in February 1945, as I have already related. In discussing the government of Poland after the war Stalin had been obdurate – and devious – in supporting the pro-Communist Polish group as against the Polish government-in-exile in London with whom the Allies had been working throughout the war. Sixteen pro-democratic Poles, some from London, assembled in Poland after Yalta for the agreed consultations between the different groups then completely disappeared. All the diplomatic protestations made by the Western powers in Moscow were received in stony silence, until finally one evening in San Francisco Molotov, the Soviet Foreign Minister, casually announced to Anthony Eden and Edward Stettinius, the US Secretary of State, that all the London Poles had been arrested. This blatant breach of the Yalta agreement was to my mind one of the earliest and clearest signals of the difficulties that were going to arise in inter-allied relationships after the war.

However, another incident at San Francisco showed how confused Western opinion still was about the Soviet

Union. The US delegation decided to call an off-the-record press briefing to warn selected American correspondents about the difficulties that were arising with the Soviet Union, but when Averell Harriman, himself a liberal in outlook as regards American-Soviet relations, cited the events in Poland, two of America's most respected media figures, Walter Lippmann and Raymond Gram Swing, walked out announcing that they would not listen to such smears of America's brave Russian allies.

Meantime the Polish seat at the conference remained empty, and, to complicate matters, the wild press columnists began to speculate that a Russian-Polish ship, the *Batory*, which had appeared in San Francisco Bay, was full of pro-Communist Poles who at a given signal would appear dramatically on the conference floor and occupy the Polish seats. In reality, as we discovered later, the Russians for safety reasons were shrewdly using the *Batory* to house their cypher-machines, whereas other delegations, including the British, were doing their cypher work in much less secure hotel bedrooms.

The second cause for conference gloom was a renewed disagreement over the system of voting in the Security Council. In the course of the committee discussions it became clear that Russia was still insisting, as they had done at Dumbarton Oaks, that the five Permanent Members, and therefore the Soviet Union itself, should have the right to vote even in cases where they themselves were party to a dispute, and even in cases where only the *peaceful* settlement of a dispute was under consideration. This would have meant power to control the agenda of the Security Council and would largely have annulled the effect of the concession that Stalin had made at Yalta. The whole San Francisco conference, and especially the smaller countries, were outraged by this attempt at great power domination, but Gromyko was adamant. In the end the conference had to mark time on this issue while a special mission consisting of Harry Hopkins and Averell Harriman, sent to Moscow by President Truman, sought to get Stalin to alter Gromyko's instructions. In the end the Russians gave way.

The third issue which threatened the conference concerned the terms of the Trusteeship Chapter in the Charter, and involved the whole future of colonialism. Britain was inevitably central to this dispute and the chosen spokesman for the non-self-governing territories (in today's parlance, the developing world) was the Philippine delegate General Carlos Romulo. Romulo was an able, articulate and sometimes inflammatory speaker. He was calling off-the-record press briefings to alert the media to the fact that at the next meeting of the Trusteeship Committee he intended to deliver a broadside against British policy. Press predictions were emanating from San Francisco about a major crisis impending in the conference.

It was at this moment that what Adam Smith might earlier have called 'an invisible hand' intervened in the San Francisco conference. On the one hand, Romulo became intrigued by a change in outlook in one of the members of his staff who had been on the verge of a breakdown but had found a new sense of calm and balance. Romulo was told that the change was due to her contacts with Moral Re-Armament, and so he became aware of the presence of Frank Buchman and his friends in San Francisco. On the other hand, a small group of delegates (including Romulo), concerned about the worsening atmosphere in the conference, had asked Frank Buchman if MRA could help in any way, for example by putting on special performances of a play called *The Forgotten Factor*. This play – which had an industrial, not a diplomatic, theme – had been one of the spearheads of MRA's morale-raising campaigns all over America and was available in San Francisco. President Truman, while still a Senator, had called it one of the most important plays produced by the war.

This was arranged and the three performances of the play were listed in the official conference diary of events. They took place in the famous private theatre of the Bohemian Club. Hundreds of delegates attended and there is no doubt that the play had an effect on many of them, perhaps most on General Romulo himself. At the fateful meeting of the Trusteeship Committee he continued to fight for his principles but the tone of his speech was very different from what had been predicted. In fact, he slipped me a brief note across the committee floor saying: 'This was the forgotten factor, wasn't it?' In the ensuing Plenary Session to endorse the Committee's recommendation his speech was again so different from earlier expectations that the British delegate, Lord Cranborne, had to amend his reply on the spur of the moment to match the new tone of Romulo's speech. The conference crisis had been dissolved and Alistair Cooke, commentator for the BBC and the *Manchester Guardian*, said that General Romulo had 'unaccountably fallen in love with the British'. This was one of the most dramatic examples I had met of the importance of the human factor in public affairs. Alexis de Tocqueville, father of modern democratic philosophy, had stated the truth clearly enough 200 years earlier: 'I am thoroughly convinced that political societies are not what their laws make them, but what they are prepared in advance to be by the feelings, the beliefs, the ideas, the habits of heart and mind of the men who compose them.'

Many times subsequently as I watched debates unfold slowly and acrimoniously in different UN bodies, I have reflected on the fact that the problems on the table were really not so complicated as the problems sitting *around* the table. But, despite de Tocqueville, no one was doing anything about them.

So although MRA had had nothing to do directly with the committees which drafted the Charter, it had had an intangible but important effect on the outcome of the conference, and when President Truman came to San Francisco for the signing of the Charter on 25th June, he met Dr Buchman and thanked him for his work.

The conference ended in a mood of optimism and much mutual congratulation and I decided to take a few days' leave before resuming my post in Washington. I set off by train with about a dozen other members of the British delegation, including some close friends, to Seattle and Vancouver, planning to take a breather in the Canadian Rockies before returning to my desk in Washington. I said goodbye to my friends at Banff, as they were due to fly back to England from Calgary. However, their RAF plane disappeared in mid-Atlantic and no wreckage was ever found. Deeply shocked, I made my way south towards Mackinac Island, where an MRA conference was taking place, and broke my journey there before continuing to Washington. On Mackinac I told Frank Buchman what had happened. He said little but immediately took me into the small island chapel where we sat in silence together.

5

New York - the UN:
'the newest show in town'

Although no decision was made at San Francisco about the site of the headquarters of the new organisation, it was agreed that a Preparatory Committee should convene in London in the autumn of 1945 to continue the work, and in October I was released from my duties in Washington and transferred back to London.

The Preparatory Commission met in Church House, the administrative headquarters of the Church of England, in the shadow of Parliament. Under the able leadership of Gladwyn Jebb, who had been a key figure in the British delegations at Dumbarton Oaks and San Francisco, it proved to be a surprisingly businesslike body and all the preparations were in fact completed in time for the first General Assembly of the United Nations to commence just across the street from Church House, in the Methodist Central Hall, Westminster, on 5th January 1946. Thus, although the UN Charter had been conceived in an opera house, it came to birth in a decidedly ecclesiastical atmosphere.

Two days after the opening in London my mother died in Scotland, and I personally once again experienced the shock of a sudden switch from euphoria to deep loss which I had felt immediately after the San Francisco conference. I took the night train from London to Glasgow. Next morning I caught a bus to the village of Killearn, 15 miles from Glasgow, where my mother had died in hospital from a brain tumour. I still remember vividly how, as we rolled along the Strathblane valley, a brilliant rainbow appeared exactly overarching the valley, an unusual event in mid-winter in our part of Scotland.

My mother was a quiet person with a strong faith. I have always known that I owed a very great deal to her. No matter how much help I have received from others, it was she who set me on the path I have been trying to follow ever since. After my mother's death my father and brother continued to live in our old family home in Glasgow while my brother, just out of the army, finished his interrupted degree in history at Glasgow University. He then followed my footsteps to Oxford and later became a journalist with *The Economist* magazine and other publications. My father eventually retired to Edinburgh and died there in 1967.

The inauguration of the UN General Assembly in London by King George VI was a moving moment. The King's ineradicable stammer and slow delivery meant that every single delegate and adviser in the vast audience listened with complete concentration – a rare occurrence in UN gatherings. The manifest sincerity of the monarch, his deep belief in the principles and purposes of the new organisation, shone through. And interestingly enough, this sincere personal attachment was confirmed eloquently 50 years later by his daughter Queen Elizabeth II in her address in Westminster Hall celebrating the UN Jubilee, when I found myself, with my wife, on the podium reserved for survivors of the San Francisco conference.

Afterwards when we were received in Buckingham Palace, it was obvious that the Queen and the Duke of Edinburgh had been well briefed about our reasons for being

present, but the Prince of Wales was more to the point.
'What I want to know,' he said, 'is what you are doing for
the United Nations in Scotland *now*.' This unexpected query
gave me a chance to pay tribute to the under-recognised
services of the late Marquess of Bute who for many years
quietly promoted and financed the work of the United
Nations Educational Trust for Scotland of which I was vice-
chairman.

One of the first tasks of the London Assembly was to
find a secretary-general for the new organisation. Everyone recognised the prime importance of this appointment
and many world celebrities were suggested – General
Eisenhower and Lester Pearson, later Prime Minister of
Canada, among them. But of course the choice had to be
made in accordance with the Charter's rule about 'the
unanimity of the five permanent members'. This meant
Russian concurrence and that was one of the chief reasons
why the ultimate victor was Trygve Lie, Foreign Minister
of Norway. It was inevitably a compromise choice. Trygve
Lie was well-meaning and hard-working but it was not
until the selection of Dag Hammarskjöld in 1953 that the
full potentialities of the post of secretary-general were displayed.

Another early task of the London Assembly was to
choose a site for the headquarters of the new organisation.
This provoked much animated debate and not a little
under-the-table lobbying. The US Government tried to
maintain a dignified stance in the debate but individual
American cities and states, led by San Francisco and California, bombarded the conference with offers and entice-
ments. The Soviet Union at the outset favoured San
Francisco, a tribute to the royal treatment we had all
received there. However, most of the European countries
favoured Geneva, pointing out that the League of Nations
buildings were immediately available for use. The Prime

Minister of New Zealand, Peter Fraser, obviously of direct
Scottish ancestry, quietly promoted the claims of Gleneagles in the Scottish Highlands where a deluxe hotel stood
empty, and it is tempting to speculate on how differently
the United Nations might have developed if it had been
conducting its business over the years in the cool, damp,
beautiful seclusion of Perthshire instead of in the frenetic
atmosphere of Manhattan.

However, it was clear from the outset that a majority of
the countries represented in London favoured the United
States as headquarters – not least because of a desire to
counter the remaining appeals for isolationism there. Even
after the basic decision in favour of America had been
made, a heated tussle went on between different American
cities, and it was only years later through the generous
intervention of the Rockefeller family that the UN headquarters began to arise on the East Side of Manhattan.

To guide the search for a site, a UN Headquarters Commission was set up at the London Assembly and its elected
chairman was Dr Stojan Gavrilović, a Yugoslav diplomat
who became a close friend of mine. When the Nazi
blitzkrieg overwhelmed Yugoslavia in April 1941,
Gavrilović – then a senior official in the Belgrade Foreign
Ministry – managed to escape with members of the government and some of the Yugoslav royal family to the
Adriatic coast where he and a few others were picked up
by a British flying boat, transferred to a Royal Navy submarine and carried to safety in Cairo. Meanwhile his wife
and young son had made their way, via Romania and
Jerusalem, to South Africa where they eventually got a
ship destined for the United States, only to be torpedoed
by a German submarine a few miles off the coast of North
Carolina. Happily, after three days in a lifeboat, they were
saved by the US Navy.

Gavrilović and I shared a common outlook on life and

I admired the efforts he made to stick to his principles while working for a Marxist government still in its most rabid phase. It was a government I was to come to know at first hand decades later, but by then its head, Marshal Tito, had mellowed considerably and his totalitarian régime was even showing signs of benignity.

The London Assembly had a double interest for me in that it was my first opportunity to make personal contact with the leaders of the new Labour Government of Clement Attlee. Those I dealt with on UN affairs were Ernest Bevin, Philip Noel-Baker, Christopher Mayhew, Sir Hartley Shawcross and Francis Williams, formerly Editor of the *Daily Herald* and then press spokesman at 10 Downing Street and with whom I had already worked at the San Francisco conference. But the greatest pleasure was to find myself working closely with Hector McNeil, then a junior minister in the Foreign Office but earlier a near-contemporary of mine at Glasgow University. Hector and I struck up a close working relationship on both sides of the Atlantic (for he was a frequent visitor to New York) in which the reserves frequently observed between politicians and civil servants had no meaning. Hector became Secretary of State for Scotland in the last phase of Attlee's Government, but he and I remained close friends until his premature death – from a stroke aboard the *Queen Mary* – in 1955; and his widow Sheila remains a good friend till the present day. Hector enjoyed what is called 'the good life', and sometimes 'the high life', and he was not in any sense an orthodox Presbyterian. But he had a sense of fairness and moral principles which led him to fight behind the scenes for a 'fair deal' not only for me but for others in Moral Re-Armament who became victims of prejudice in some sections of the Foreign Office, Whitehall and Westminster.

It had been the hope that the London Assembly, coming

so soon after the end of the war, would concern itself mainly with organisational matters and that the UN would get off to a smooth start. But this was not to be. Within weeks acrimonious debates broke out in the Assembly and in the Security Council over the civil war in Greece, the removal of Dutch troops from Indonesia and the withdrawal of Soviet troops from Northern Persia. Moreover in each of these disputes the Russians were ranged against the Western powers. Whether we liked it or not, the Cold War had already begun.

In London I was formally offered the post of First Secretary on the staff of Sir Alexander Cadogan, Britain's first resident representative to the UN in New York, with special responsibility for public relations. I accepted without hesitation and we set off for New York in early February 1946.

When we landed, we were persuaded by the chief American delegate, Ed Stettinius, previously Truman's Secretary of State, to transfer to the Savoy Plaza Hotel on 5th Avenue and 59th Street ('my family hotel', Stettinius called it), and we were so well treated there that we stayed on for the next four years. In addition, the Cadogans, like many other UN delegates, had a country house on Long Island and I lodged there time and again, almost as one of their family.

Cadogan was a spare, compact, handsome figure, quiet, witty and invariably even-tempered. Only by reading his wartime diaries (*The Diaries of Sir Alexander Cadogan 1938-45*, edited by David Dilks, Cassell 1971) does one discover the seething exasperation over human follies that lay beneath his calm exterior. And only on the golf-course, where his form was as unpredictable as his appearances in the Security Council were the opposite, did he really let himself go!

I was lucky to be groomed in multilateral diplomacy by

an expert in the art. After a distinguished early career which took him to Constantinople, Vienna, the League of Nations and Peking, Cadogan became head of the Foreign Office in January 1938 and he continued as Permanent Under-Secretary until the end of the Second World War, a gruelling experience by any measurement. It meant that he was in daily contact with Churchill and Eden, both high-voltage personalities, plus the British military Chiefs of Staff and the leaders of the European governments-in-exile whose territories were overrun by Hitler but who continued to function from London. Yet he ended the war still holding the trust and respect of almost all these *prima donnas*.

He had been at Churchill's side, as his closest civilian aide, at practically all the wartime conferences between Churchill, Roosevelt and Stalin, and was the principal architect of the Atlantic Charter which had been drafted in haste on board ship in Placentia Bay, Newfoundland, during the first historic meeting of Churchill and Roosevelt in August 1941.

I believe I learned more from Cadogan than from any other person in my professional career. His unassuming manner and tendency towards understatement, coupled with his exceptional experiences, made him an even better teacher by osmosis than resort to exhortation or admonishment would have done.

He was not a prophet or far-seeing statesman. He conceived his job as being to 'keep the show on the road', if one can borrow a metaphor from the theatre where unrestrained egos are even more plentiful than in international diplomacy.

One thing I learned from him was the importance of going to the heart of any problem instead of wasting time and energy (and frequently emotion) on peripheral issues. Cadogan had developed the art of spotting the essential minimum that required to be done at any given time in any tangled situation. That was probably what enabled him to retain his sanity and good sense through all the trials and tribulations of the war years. It was typical of him that he would normally type out his own speeches for the Security Council in New York on his portable typewriter, based on telegraphed instruction from London, whereas today most political celebrities would have banks of speech-writers preparing repeated drafts of their eventual 'heartfelt' utterances.

I also learned much from Cadogan's imperturbability, the other quality which had helped him survive the war tensions. The most dramatic recorded example of that concerned an incident on a converted bomber in which he was flying to a wartime conference. Near the end of the flight, for some unknown reason, part of the bomb-bay structure dropped off, forcing the pilot to lower altitude and causing gusts of chilly air to invade the improvised cabin. These developments naturally caused a commotion amongst the air-crew and the other passengers. Cadogan, however, remained seated, moved his spectacles to the point of his nose so that he could see better what was going on, and calmly continued reading his briefs. I learned a lot from him, but never quite reached such levels of unflappability.

I can remember only one occasion when Cadogan's professional cool deserted him. It was when he came out of a telephone booth in the delegates' lounge at the UN headquarters and said: 'This is the limit. Uncle Ernie (Bevin) has discovered that he can use his bedside telephone to send me instructions direct. He has just changed our policy on Palestine!'

It is a curious fact that this cautious imperturbability was a quality which Cadogan shared in some measure with his Soviet opposite number, Andrei Gromyko.

Allowances having been made for the brinkmanship and verbal pyrotechnics characteristic of the Cold War, one could not visualise either of them, accidentally or deliberately, pressing the panic button.

Lady Cadogan's relations with Gromyko, her frequent dinner companion at UN functions, was another matter altogether. Lady Theo, daughter of the Earl of Gosford, was a gracious hostess, with an air of insouciance and a professed incapacity to understand international politics. Yet her apparent non sequiturs and casual shafts of wit left her neighbours wondering; and I suspect that Gromyko, if pressed on what he really thought about Lady Theo, might have borrowed Churchill's words on Russian policy and described her as 'a riddle, wrapped in a mystery, inside an enigma'.

Cadogan – because of his work at Dumbarton Oaks and San Francisco – was widely recognised even amongst his fellow delegates in New York as one of the foremost authorities on the Charter. This fact, plus the prestige that still rubbed off on the British delegation because of Britain's war record, made my job as a public relations officer relatively easy (except when the issue of Palestine came up!) and we came in for quite a bit of favourable comment. The chief UN correspondent of the *New York Post*, not known for its pro-British sentiments, wrote: 'Mackenzie has become celebrated as the author of more good news breaks than any other single source in the United Nations corral. If something was going on, standard operating procedure was to "get Archie". Because if Archie knew and he could tell, and usually he knew and could, the story made the next edition. ...... His freedom of expression was supported by his boss, Sir Alexander Cadogan, who realised as few diplomats have that big news can't be kept a secret for very long.'

Funnily enough, these sentiments were echoed 50 years

later in a private letter to my wife from Nancy Maclennan, who had been a *New York Times* correspondent at UN headquarters in the 1940s and who subsequently by marriage became the Countess of Enniskillen. She wrote: 'Archie was in my opinion the prototype of what any government could desire in its information officers. So fair .... and always knowing to whom he might safely entrust whatever might be off the record. It was such a pleasure dealing with him from my New York Times portfolio.'

The expectations of the American public as regards the UN were at first very high. It was, after all, 'the newest show in town'. The New Yorkers were almost as hospitable as San Francisco had been in the previous year. Social invitations were showered on the UN newcomers – to dinners, theatres and country weekends. The delegates were treated as minor celebrities. It was all very enjoyable, although my own closest encounter with stardom was brief – and accidental. I was coming out of 30 Rockefeller Plaza and the rain was teeming down. The queue for taxis was miserably trying to shelter itself under real or improvised umbrellas. I was in the second category and was paying little attention to the people around me. When my turn came, I shouted to the taxi-driver: '166 East Seventy-First Street, please,' and prepared to dive into the cab when the next person in the queue said: 'Oh, I'm going up the Eastside too, to the Carlyle. Could I possibly share your cab to get out of the rain?'

I could only say yes and moved over to allow an elegant youngish lady to squeeze onto the seat beside me. After mutually bemoaning the awful weather, my companion said: 'You must be from England.' I indicated that in a general sense I was, although there were differences between Scotland and England. It quickly became clear that she was very knowledgeable about both sides of the Atlantic and we chatted amicably about places we knew and about the UN, as the taxi-cab sped up town. As we reached the Carlyle Hotel, my companion prepared to get out and said: 'It's been so nice talking to you. I hope we'll meet again. My name is Gertrude Lawrence.'

Gertrude Lawrence was then the toast of Broadway, playing in *Blithe Spirit* with Noel Coward, but I had completely failed to recognise her. All I could think to say was: 'My name is Archie Mackenzie,' and the star stepped out of my life.

In those early days crowds queued to get into the UN buildings and to attend meetings. And with the arrival of television, UN delegates became full-blown public celebrities. The whole conduct of diplomacy was being revolutionised. From the old-time secrecy – evident at the Hot Springs and Dumbarton Oaks conferences – we had moved to what might be better called goldfish-bowl diplomacy with all its advantages and drawbacks. Even the shape of the Security Council table at Lake Success, site of the UN's temporary headquarters, was decided with television in mind. Logically it should have been a round table where delegates talked directly at each other. But in fact it was made as a wide arc just to suit the TV cameras. We were moving closer than ever before towards the 'open covenants of peace openly arrived at' which Woodrow Wilson had proclaimed as the proper goal of diplomacy in the 20th century. When the Korean War broke out in 1951 American audiences for the first time saw the issues of peace and war being decided before their eyes. It was said that the British delegate – by then Gladwyn Jebb, Cadogan's successor – had a higher audience rating than Bob Hope.

Such unexpected and unprecedented popularity did not last for long. However, the UN did launch an early initiative to promote the principles of freedom of information – central to open diplomacy – on a world-wide basis. It set

up a sub-commission on Freedom of Information in 1947
to prepare for a world conference on Freedom of Information to be held in Geneva in 1948. The British nominee
to the sub-commission was a well-known London journalist, Robin Cruikshank, editor of the *News Chronicle*.
Unfortunately he fell ill at the very last moment and I was
unexpectedly nominated to take his place and found
myself operating amongst a group of about 20 senior
media figures from around the world. Fortunately things
went reasonably well and the left-inclined New York
weekly, *The New Republic*, was kind enough to say:
'Mackenzie is easily the ablest man on the sub-commission
despite the fact that he was called in at the last minute. He
has been responsible for more compromise solutions than
anybody else and his quick perception has saved days of
work.'

The sub-commission held two ten-day sessions in New
York and was expected to be a fairly uneventful affair,
screwing together the nuts and bolts for the World Conference in Geneva. However, between the first and second
sessions events were hurrying on in Europe as a result of
the Cold War and in particular the dramatic overturn of
democracy in Czechoslovakia. One result of this was that
the Czech nominee to the sub-commission, a well-known
liberal editor called Lev Sychrava, failed to turn up for the
second session. He was a quiet, dignified man, a survivor
of Buchenwald, with an unblemished record as a champion of democracy in his own country. We had become
good friends at the first session and so I felt deeply his
unexplained and suspicious non-appearance at the second
session. I led the protests and demands for an explanation
that gathered strength around the conference table to the
discomfiture of the Soviet representative. I fear our
protests achieved very little. Lev Sychrava never appeared
again on the international scene, but at one throw I had

become very personally involved in the painful consequences of the Cold War.

The Sub-Commission inevitably produced many barbed
exchanges with the Soviet delegate across the table, Jakob
Lomakin, but I tried my best to maintain friendly personal
relations with him at the same time. After one heated
debate I said to him privately at the end of the meeting:
'Look here, we seem to be getting nowhere on the present
basis. I admit we British are not perfect. Tell me, are you
Russians ever sinners?'

There was a lengthy silence as he figured how to
respond to this unexpected sally. Finally he came out with
the historic response: 'I do not think we have that word in
our language.'

Lomakin was also serving as Soviet Consul-General in
New York City and some time later he found himself on
all the front pages when a Russian girl employed in his
household staff jumped out of a third-storey window at
the Consulate building. She was rescued by the New York
police and soon afterwards Lomakin also – like Sychrava
– disappeared from the international scene.

The Sub-Commission duly completed its preparatory
work and the World Conference on Freedom of Information opened in Geneva in March 1948. I was seconded to
the British team and was glad to find myself working
closely with Hector McNeil as leader of the British delegation and with the chairman of the conference who was
General Carlos Romulo, now Foreign Minister of The
Philippines, with whom I had had such interesting interac-
tions at the San Francisco conference.

I also recall during the conference an interesting evening
spent *tête-à-tête* in a Geneva restaurant with the celebrated
author Ian Fleming, creator of the James Bond character,
and another close journalist friend, Henry Brandon of the
London *Sunday Times* – such were the levels of interest

and hope aroused even among the *cognoscenti* by United Nations initiatives in those early days.

The Geneva conference, though handicapped by the Cold War, at least laid the ground work for subsequent valuable work by the United Nations in the field of freedom of information, but before its close I had been urgently summoned back to New York to tackle more incendiary matters, at the Special Assembly called to attend to the future of Palestine.

Palestine was without question the biggest issue with which the UN had to deal up to that time. The Security Council had been occupied with endless and increasingly bitter debate over Cold War issues. But both the Western powers and the Soviet Union were protected by their veto rights, and neither side wished to precipitate an atomic war. So inevitably these debates ended in little more than words and threats. Palestine was different. The British Government, the mandatory power, wanted to get rid of the burden of Palestine altogether. For her own selfish reasons Britain therefore did what was perfectly permissible and indeed logical under the UN Charter: she announced a date of withdrawal and handed the whole problem over to the United Nations to solve.

In a Jewish-dominated city like New York, this was a sensation. To the United States Government, under strong Jewish pressure, it was an embarrassment. To most of the UN members it was a headache that they wished would go away. And to the UN secretariat itself it was almost too big a challenge to cope with.

In London the decision to get rid of our responsibilities in Palestine brought a certain relief from the almost unbearable situation where we were being reviled and shot at by both Jews and Arabs. But for the British delegation in New York the perspective was somewhat different. We found ourselves very much on the front line and criticised

on all sides. The Jews were convinced there was a hidden
trap. The Arabs were unprepared and apprehensive. The
Americans were embarrassed. So were the Russians. And
most of the smaller members of the UN, plus the UN Secretariat, were irritated at having this hot potato thrown
into their hands before they were ready to cope with it.

In charge of public relations, and facing a unanimously
hostile or suspicious press, I found myself in a no-win situation. The only thing I could do was to draw on the
reserves of trust that I had built up personally with the
media representatives, in the hope of getting a square
deal, and to be as straight and honest as I could. It was a
difficult time and, as everyone knows, the UN has proved
incapable of finding a satisfactory solution to the problem
till the present time – over 50 years later.

Since these early dramas, the United Nations has continued to occupy a central place in the unfolding history of the
second half of the 20th century and promises to do the same
in the 21st century. Virtually no member-state is satisfied
with it: yet no one wants to leave it. Its membership has
exploded from 51 to 199 and the first step of each territory
on gaining (or claiming) independence is to apply for UN
membership.

It has few clear-cut victories to claim: it has had many
failures, many fudges and many botched jobs. Public and
governmental support for it has declined. Its debts have
soared and some of its most powerful members, notably
the US Government, have been very negligent contribu-
tors.

The end of the Cold War and the total collapse of the
Russian Communist regime in 1989-91 should have –
could have – been a chance to reinvigorate and transform
the United Nations, but despite torrents of supporting
words, this did not happen. The chance was missed. The
fact was that the member-states, and not least the West-

ern powers, were unwilling to give more power to the UN, unwilling to cede more sovereignty to it. Individual governments did not trust it sufficiently to give it more decision-making powers and enforcement capacities on vital matters. Its record of fudge, of delay, and of down-right incompetence and waste, was too great. Effort after effort at reform ran into the sand.

So the world went on changing ceaselessly, and in many respects at ever greater speeds, but the United Nations remained virtually unchanged with the same basic consti-tution as it had been given in 1945. The UN is essentially an intergovernmental organisation, without supra-national powers, and it seems likely to remain that way. Governments may be willing, usually reluctantly, to hand over limited parts of their sovereign powers to smaller international groups of like-minded states, but there is very little sign of any increasing willingness to share powers with a world body.

The Charter drafted at San Francisco in 1945 has obvi-ous imperfections, but if it were to be abandoned for any unforeseen and deeply regrettable reason, I think that, like Humpty Dumpty, it would prove much more difficult – if not impossible – to put it together again. It has served the world community well and we should be thinking of improvements, not alternatives. Many revisions (for example, to enlarge the Security Council) have been, and still are, under active discussion though very few have been accepted.

My personal wish would be that we could either elimi-nate or drastically revise Article 2.7 which says: 'Nothing contained in the present Charter shall authorise the United Nations to intervene in matters which are essentially within the domestic jurisdiction of any state ...'

To my mind this clause has been like a millstone around the UN's neck ever since its inception. But it is important to realise that it was not a restriction imposed by any one state or group of states. It was a restriction that was sought by a great many countries at San Francisco – by great powers wanting to protect themselves against irresponsible interference by small powers; by Latin Americans protecting themselves against their giant neighbour to the north; by members of the British Empire apprehensive of interference from London; by South Africans mindful of their apartheid philosophy; by Australians mindful of their white Australia policy; and so on *ad infinitum*.

It was all very understandable, but the net effect of the clause was a weakening of the UN structure from the beginning. The appeal to Article 2.7 has been too often the last appeal of the wrongdoer. But in the closing decades of the 20th century world conditions were changing so rapidly and so indisputably that, with the growth of globalisation and the blatant denial of human rights by governments in so many parts of the globe, the limitations of Article 2.7 were deemed to be unjust, and even a cloak for genocide. In recent years the clause has therefore been rather more honoured in the breach than in the observance. (How much is now 'essentially' within domestic jurisdiction in a global village?) Yet the clause is still appealed to time and again to prevent UN action even in Europe, and I strongly feel that it has outlived its usefulness – at least in its present form.

I left Cadogan's staff in New York on transfer to the Foreign Office in October 1949 on the very day that the news broke in the United Nations that the Soviet Union had exploded its first atomic bomb. So my departure was scarcely noticed. I was to return to the UN 23 years later in a quite different capacity: but of that, more anon.

6

Bangkok – discovering Asia

In June 1951, when I was working in the American Department in the Foreign Office, the authorities announced that my next job would be as First Secretary in the British Embassy in Bangkok. To me, so far used only to the hubbub of Washington, New York and the Foreign Office itself, this sounded an odd idea.

Tourists had not yet heard of Thailand. I had never been further east than Switzerland. British atlases were still calling the country Siam rather than Thailand. It almost seemed like banishment to the edge of the world.

Moreover, at that moment Thailand was staging one of its periodic domestic coups. The London papers announced that the road on which the British Embassy was situated had been strafed by gunfire between the Air Force headquarters at one end of the road and the Navy establishment at the other. By a fluke, an Air Force plane had dropped a bomb down the funnel of the warship, moored in mid-stream, in which the Navy were holding the Prime Minister imprisoned. In the ensuing chaos, he swam ashore and resumed charge of the government. Tentatively I asked the Foreign Office if they would like me to delay my departure until the dust had settled, but their reply was unequivocal: 'No. Get there sooner if you can.'

Upon my arrival in Bangkok, where I knew not one single soul, I was met by an Embassy car and driver but, outside Bangkok airport, the car had to stop to permit a herd of elephants to cross the main road (which today has become an eight-lane highway jammed with traffic and polluted by exhaust fumes). As I watched the unaccustomed scene in 1951, I said silently to myself: 'Mackenzie, you are in a new world.'

Life in Bangkok was then much simpler and more leisurely than it later became. Canal traffic was more common than speedway traffic. The old-world beauty of the city had not been threatened by commercialisation. I stayed initially at the old Oriental Hotel on the bank of the Menam Chao Phraya river which dissects Bangkok and I quickly became fascinated by the pulsating river life, the non-stop manoeuvrings of everything from tiny sampans to ocean-going craft. Haunted by the ghosts of Somerset Maugham and other early literary travellers, the old Oriental was a much simpler hostelry than the deluxe new Oriental which occupies the same space today. My room had no air-conditioning, only an electric fan, a punkah which lazily turned at ceiling level, and I slept in a box-bed surrounded by mosquito netting. Soon, however, I was moved into a small house near the Embassy, complete with a picturesque lily-pond. Orchids clung to the trees. Bougainvillaea and frangipani abounded. The food and fruit were exotic but delicious. Despite my ignorance, it was not difficult to appreciate my surroundings.

Not long after my own arrival, we received a new and very able ambassador, Sir Geoffrey Wallinger. As his Head of Chancery, or adjutant, I owed a lot to the trust and friendship which he and his French wife showed to me.

The Ambassador's presentation of credentials to the King in the Royal Palace in Bangkok was an unforgettable experience for more than one reason. Every country has its own protocol regulations for such ceremonies, always formal and dignified, in Buckingham Palace no less than elsewhere.

The Royal Palace in Bangkok is a vision of white marble, gilded columns and delicately carved roofs. The marble floors are covered with precious rugs. Our Embassy party, in white diplomatic uniforms, was lined up behind the Ambassador in order of seniority – about a dozen in all. Our instructions, as I recall, were on entering the throne hall to advance two paces and bow: then advance six more paces and bow for the second time: finally to advance three more paces and make a third bow. By then it was calculated that the Ambassador would be within speaking range of the monarch.

The ceremony itself was brief and simple. Sir Geoffrey handed over his written credentials from the Queen and a brief conversation followed *tête-à-tête* with the shy young King, Phumiphon Adundet. We were then ready to depart, but this was where the hazards began to surface. Thai protocol dictated that one should never turn one's back on royalty and so the withdrawal procedure, similar to our entry, had to be carried out backwards. The colleague immediately behind me had the misfortune to catch his heel on the edge of a rug on the marble floor. He stumbled momentarily and I inadvertently ruffled the rug even more: so for a brief moment there was a real possibility that the entire British Embassy would disappear in a heap, like collapsing dominoes, with the ambassador on top. However we reached the safety of the door more or less erect, and gratefully saw it closing in front of us.

I was extremely lucky in establishing my own personal links with the royal circle through a good friend in England, Barbara Ivimy, who had been at Oxford with a junior Thai princess studying there in the 1920s. In this way, at an early stage in my time in Bangkok, I had the privilege to meet Prince Dhani Niwat who had served as Regent in 1948-50 until the young King's return from his educational sojourn in Switzerland. Prince Dhani had himself been at Oxford and was a man of wide learning, great charm and even greater humility. To sit at his feet (almost literally in Thai style) was like attending a tutorial with an exquisitely polite Oxford don. From him, starting from scratch, I began to discover something about Siamese history and the riches of Siamese culture. In due course he invited me to become Secretary of the Siam Society, the main channel of cultural discussions between Thai intellectuals and foreigners resident in Bangkok; and this in turn resulted in my becoming editor of the two anniversary volumes published in 1954, consisting of papers selected from the Siam Society's journals over the previous 50 years. These volumes remain today as valuable source material for scholars of South-East Asian history and culture.

Exactly three weeks after my arrival in Bangkok my office phone rang and a Thai voice said, 'Mr Mackenzie, I have just got back from Geneva with the Thai delegation to the International Labour Organisation conference. We met friends of yours at the Moral Re-Armament conference centre at Caux and they asked us to give you greetings.'

The new MRA conference centre at Caux-sur-Montreux, high above the Lake of Geneva, came into its own in the late Forties. The Caux Palace, originally one of the grand hotels of *La Belle Epoque*, had fallen on hard times and had been used as housing for refugees and interned prisoners-of-war: but in 1946 it was bought by private Swiss citizens – in many cases at great personal sacrifice – and offered to Buchman for his work, as a gesture of gratitude for Switzerland's having escaped the war. So Caux became a centre for European reconstruction and a meeting place for wartime enemies. I knew from my days in

Washington that many US congressmen had also made their way there, and there can be no doubt that Buchman's assiduous efforts at this time had a definite effect on congressional attitudes when the crucial votes came on the Marshall Plan in 1947-8. In the Fifties statesmen and ordinary people from all over the world flocked to the annual summer conferences held at Caux, and were there able to meet and discuss freely, in an atmosphere of reconciliation and constructive exchange. Many of the delegates to the annual International Labour Organisation conference in Geneva made visits to Caux at that time, as they still do today.

The Thai delegation of four who made contact with me in this unexpected phonecall consisted of the Minister of Commerce, a civil servant, a trade union leader and a journalist. And in this way, as a young untutored diplomat still feeling very much alone in a strange land, I suddenly found doors had opened to some of the main streams of Thai life. It was like manna from heaven.

Each of these four men became a personal friend and the trade unionist, Sang Phathanothai, closest of all. He turned out to be not only president of the Thai Trade Union Movement but a special confidant of Prime Minister Pibulsonggram and through him, though I was a newcomer, I soon had direct access to the prime ministerial household – sometimes to the envy of other intelligence-gatherers. Sang was a gregarious, merry and energetic character, used to carrying out special missions for the Prime Minister, some of a secretive and rather dubious character. When he announced to the Prime Minister that as a result of his contacts with MRA in Switzerland he had decided to clean up his life and live by absolute moral standards, the news was greeted with some incredulity. 'I know you,' said the Prime Minister. 'These resolutions will not last a month.' But in fact Sang's decisions, no doubt with many a slip, governed his life until he died.

His life had many twists and turns. Later in the 1950s, when Pibulsonggram was ousted from office by a more right-wing military junta (which coincided roughly with the rise of McCarthyism in the USA), Sang came under suspicion as being allegedly pro-Communist. He was imprisoned for several years but, in typical Thai style, he still found ways to send his children to be educated abroad: two to China and his oldest son to America!

In China his daughter Sirin and his younger son were more or less adopted by Prime Minister Chou En-lai and grew up in the privileged and securely guarded prime ministerial quarters. Sirin, a vivacious and talented youngster, was nicknamed 'the Dragon's Pearl' by Chou En-lai himself, and in the 1990s wrote a best-selling book recounting her Chinese experience including her harrowing times during the Cultural Revolution. (*The Dragon's Pearl*, Simon & Schuster 1994) In 1983 I heard her make an interesting tribute to her father at a dinner for two senior Japanese businessmen who had come to Bangkok to explore the possibilities of building an overhead railway to ease the city's infamous traffic jams. Halfway through the dinner, Sirin announced to the guests: 'Whatever you may think about MRA, I know that when my father linked up with MRA, he stopped ill-treating my mother.'

Sang was also my door-opener to the Buddhist world, not a realm over-frequented by young British diplomats. Through him I became an accepted visitor to Wat Mahatat, one of the largest temples in Bangkok and site of the Buddhist priests' training college. The head of Wat Mahatat was Sang's friend, Phra Bimolodharm. He would receive and join in discussions with every MRA delegation visiting Bangkok and he personally attended numerous MRA assemblies in Europe and in the USA. Like Sang, he suffered when Thailand came under a right-wing dictatorship and was demoted and rebuked for his allegedly communistic sympathies. Eventually, however, he was reinstated as joint Primate of Thailand, and throughout his persecution he never renounced his links with MRA.

In January 1952 the first MRA conference was held in Thailand, largely on the joint initiative of Sang Phathanothai and Phya Mahai Sawarn, the Minister of Commerce and leader of the ILO delegation. It was mainly significant because it brought a Burmese delegation to Bangkok at a time when Thai-Burmese relations were still strained following the war.

Despite sharing a common religion and a similar climate, there are centuries of rivalry and even enmity between the two countries. In the 17th and 18th centuries Burma tended to be the stronger kingdom and the sacking of Thailand's ancient capital Ayuthia by Burmese invaders in the 17th century still lives in Thai memories. (It led to the transfer of the capital downstream to the port of Bangkok.)

Fortuitously, amongst the visitors from Rangoon who came to the 1952 conference was Daw Nyein Tha, a prominent Burmese educator who had been one of Frank Buchman's first and lifelong colleagues in South-East Asia and who had travelled widely with him and his associates. Ma Mi, as she was popularly called, by her grace, humour and humility completely won the affection of the Thais. On meeting the Prime Minister she announced that she had come to make restitution for the destruction of Ayuthia and of the sacred elephants there. She thereupon presented Prime Minister Pibulsonggram with a tiny pea-sized elephant carved in ivory. The Prime Minister caught the spirit of the gesture and from then on Ma Mi became an unofficial 'aunt' in the Pibulsonggram family home.

From these very simple beginnings a new warmth was gradually breathed into Burmese-Thai relations and in ensuing years Prime Minister Pibulsonggram and U Nu, the Burmese Prime Minister, exchanged friendly visits.

In 1952, on the initiative of Phya Mahai Sawarn, a past President of the Bangkok Chamber of Commerce, Thailand sent five tons of rice as a gift – delivered free to Genoa port – for use at the MRA conference at Caux, when many foodstuffs were still in short supply in Europe. This gift was repeated for several years and helped to inspire other countries to contribute supplies for use at MRA's European conferences.

Later in that year Thailand was invited to send a delegation to an international MRA conference in Sri Lanka, marking the opening of Frank Buchman's bid to influence the leadership of the new Asia that was emerging from the struggles for independence in India, Pakistan and other South-East Asian countries. The Prime Minister personally nominated a six-man delegation of senior officials led by the Speaker of the Thai Parliament, and I took a few days' leave to accompany the party. It was arranged that we would fly by BOAC Comet to Singapore and from there to Colombo. However, when we assembled at Bangkok Airport we were aghast to learn that the Comet was running late and that, because of monsoon storms over Thailand, the pilot had decided to bypass Bangkok and was flying direct from Calcutta to Singapore. Faced with this crisis, I summoned up what eloquence I could and explained to the BOAC manager at the airport in crystal-clear language that if this happened BOAC's reputation would be mud as far as the Thai government was concerned. Either panic or divine help must have given wings to my entreaties for within half an hour we were told that the Comet was being re-routed and would land at Bangkok after all. I can remember clambering aboard the plane in a monsoon downpour, but when we prepared to disembark at Singapore I was astonished to see a red carpet and an official reception party on the tarmac. It quickly became clear that the Bangkok message about the change of flight plans had been so dramatic that it had convinced the Singapore authorities that the Prime Minister of Thailand himself was on the Comet accompanied by the British Ambassador. There was scarcely time to unscramble the signals before we were on our way to Sri Lanka.

To the credit of the Singapore authorities it should be said that I have no recollection of any complaint being registered because of the mix-up: and of course at the Bangkok end no damage was done at all to Thai-Singapore relations, nor even to the reputation of British diplomacy.

The Thai delegation participated fully in the Colombo conference, which was one of Thailand's first opportunities to be associated with a pan-Asian initiative since the end of the Second World War in which Thailand – thanks to Japanese *force majeure* – had been forced to play a less-than-glorious part.

After the Colombo conference Frank Buchman and his travelling group of 200, drawn from over a dozen countries, moved over to India and spent several months touring the country, presenting a series of plays expressing MRA's philosophy, and holding meetings large and small with people from all walks of life. One of the most memorable events of the tour was a ceremony in Jaipur House in New Delhi where Frank Buchman was officially presented by the West German Minister, his French colleague beside him, with the decoration he had been awarded by the German government for his efforts to heal the bitterness rampant in Europe after the Second World War, and to build co-operation between France and Germany in particular. (France similarly honoured Buchman.) It was an unusual event and its significance was not lost on the Indian government officials and local diplomats who were present.

Buchman's Asian initiative did not produce the dramatic
reconciliations at official level that had occurred in
Germany and France after the War, but it did sow seeds
which bore rich fruit in ensuing years and led, amongst
many other things, to the establishment of MRA's Asian
conference and training centre at Panchgani in Maharash-
tra which is still flourishing today.

Meantime in Bangkok, the importance of Thailand's
post-war role as a base of Western influence was becoming
clearer. She had escaped much of the physical destruction
which Burma had suffered during the war. She was free
from the new destruction which was spreading across
Indo-China as the French struggled in vain to maintain
their controlling role. And she was free from the insurrec-
tion that had already engulfed Malaysia. Thailand's geographical position in relation to Malaysia gave her an
added importance in British eyes. Thailand's southern
provinces could be, and often were, safe havens for the
pro-Communist guerrilla forces. It therefore became
extremely important for Britain – primarily through our
Embassy in Bangkok – to reach understandings with the
Thai authorities about the sharing of sensitive intelligence
information.

For all these reasons the Bangkok Embassy increasingly
became a busier and more interesting place, and my job
with it. For a few weeks in 1953 I had even found myself
acting as Her Majesty's Chargé d'Affaires because of an
unexpected interregnum when the Embassy found itself
without both an ambassador and a counsellor. This meant
dealing directly with the American Ambassador, who happened then to be the celebrated but controversial General
'Wild Bill' Donovan, former head of OSS, America's intelligence agency during the Second World War. I must say
that, although so much his junior in years and in experience, I have never been treated more considerately than I

was in our discussions on the shifts in Western policy that were becoming urgently necessary because of the rise of Communist China.

By mid-1954 I realised that my posting in Thailand was inevitably nearing an end and, despite my initial misgivings, I found myself reluctant to leave. I had learnt a lot, though it was brought home to me soon after my return to London how much more I still had to learn. I had valued the services of the young Chinese servant looking after my house, and I had encouraged him to develop as best I could. When I noticed stacks of bicycles periodically appearing outside my front gate at lunchtime, I asked him whom they belonged to.

'Oh,' he said, 'these are my friends coming for the English lessons I give in the garden shed.'

'Well done, Wong,' I replied, and offered to supply some English school books from the British Council library if that would be helpful. In London, however, I found a slightly frosty letter from the Embassy saying that they were sorry to have to tell me that the police had informed them that my garden shed had been doubling as an active gambling den, and Wong had disappeared.

Undoubtedly I had been in Thailand at a good time. I knew 'unspoiled' Bangkok when the tempo of life was closer to the movements on the *klongs* (canals) than to the hectic pace of 'life in the fast lane' for which Bangkok had become famous – or infamous – by the 1990s. There was an ease of relationship with the Thai people, who had never been subjected to colonialism, which was absent from social relations in many other newly independent countries, and there was a new openness to the West because of the geopolitical conditions in the rest of South-East Asia which I have already explained. In that developing partnership with the West, the British Embassy certainly played its part. And in the process I personally had made friendships which have lasted for decades.

Looking back, I would have difficulty in saying whether my desk activities or my extra-curricular activities – contacts with the Buddhist world, academia, royal circles, etc – were more significant. In fact, they merged time and again, and the one sure thing is that the policy-makers in the Foreign Office received a much richer stream of information about trends in Thailand than they might have anticipated.

Queen's College, Oxford High Street, 1938 – author third from right. 'My generation at Oxford lived out its student days against a background of international turbulence.'
Inset: Author in his college football colours 1937-39

UN conference at San Francisco, 1945 – 'the most remarkable and enjoyable inter-governmental conference I have ever attended'

Isaiah Berlin: 'Isaiah's reports ... were considered essential reading in Whitehall by everyone from Churchill downwards ... he later acquired a reputation as one of the sages of the 20th century.'
Photo © Clive Barda

With Lord Halifax at San Francisco, 1945. 'Lord Halifax ended the war as a much-admired figure all over America.'   Photo © MRA Productions

With Hector McNeil, Minister at the Foreign Office, 1947, UN New York – 'Hector and I struck up a close working relationship on both sides of the Atlantic.'

With US (Prof Zechariah Chafee) and Soviet (Jakob Lomakin) representatives at UN Sub-Commission on Freedom of Information, 1947

Photo: Leo Roenthal

With Sir Alexander Cadogan (right) and Sir
Hartley Shawcross at UN 1948 – 'I learned
more from Cadogan than from any other
person in my professional career.'

With Prime Minister Pibulsonggram of
Thailand, Zurich 1955
Photo © MRA Productions

With Frank Buchman and Rajmohan Gandhi, Mackinac Island 1958, for Buchman's 80th
birthday – 'Buchman's gift was to take ancient truths and rearticulate them in
arresting ways for contemporary society.'

7

Cyprus – message from 'murder mile'

In September 1954, while I was serving as assistant head of the North American Department in the Foreign Office, I was whisked out to Cyprus almost literally at a moment's notice because of my United Nations' experience. The reasons for the surprise move were twofold: firstly a gaffe in the House of Commons by the Minister of State for Colonial Affairs, Henry Hopkinson, who unwisely said that some parts of the British Commonwealth would 'never be suitable' for independence, among them Cyprus; and secondly, the decision of the Greek Government to bring their campaign for the union of Cyprus with Greece, *Enosis*, before the United Nations. The Hopkinson 'never never' speech infuriated Greek opinion, both on the mainland and on the island. Already a fiery movement for *Enosis* had been stimulated in Cyprus by Archbishop Makarios, starting in 1950 with a church-organised plebiscite which resulted in a 96 per cent vote in its favour.

This placed the colonial government in Nicosia in great difficulty. Their function was to govern the island and fend off interference. They had no special competence in international affairs, and in London a policy of non-interference by outsiders was also dominant. But the fact was, whether Nicosia and London liked it or not, Cyprus had become an international issue.

Just before leaving London I got news that the Governor in Cyprus had appointed a new government information officer by the name of Lawrence Durrell, not yet the literary celebrity that he was later to become. Whether Durrell's appointment and my own had been co-ordinated behind the scenes between the Foreign Office and the Government of Cyprus I was never sure, but there was a certain complementarity about the two appointments. Durrell certainly knew the Greek mentality intimately, as his book *Bitter Lemons* later showed, but he knew nothing about the United Nations which was now directly involved. I, on the other hand, knew little about Greece or Cyprus but I did know the United Nations. We therefore could and did supplement one another, though Durrell's highly unbureaucratic approach to problems sometimes caused minor complications. On one thing, however, we quickly agreed, namely the difficult position of salesmen when they have nothing much to sell. British policy, both in London and Nicosia, was still on the defensive and the Greek-sponsored campaign for *Enosis* was moving ahead rapidly. A month after I reached Cyprus – as we now know – General Grivas, a fanatical Hellenist who was destined to plague the British till his death in 1974, arrived secretly at night, after a stormy crossing from the island of Rhodes in a small caique. Arms and supplies were also arriving clandestinely from Greece, and Grivas immediately began organising his armed force known as Eoka. Eoka were committed to a programme of guerrilla warfare and sabotage of governmental installations which continued in the event for nearly four years.

My own job in these circumstances was not easy. I had to explain as best I could what was happening at the United Nations and calm down the wilder stories and predictions which were being disseminated by the excitable Cypriot and Greek media. I had also to brief the growing body of international journalists who were arriving on the island as the sense of crisis grew. Simultaneously I had to keep London and New York informed of swings of public opinion, not only on Cyprus but in the surrounding region. I therefore had to visit Greece, Turkey, Lebanon and Egypt. And I also had to ensure that the Turkish-Cypriot viewpoint was not forgotten while trying to prevent it from becoming another disruptive and explosive factor. But most tricky of all was how to inject into official circles, in London as well as Nicosia, the idea that our own policies needed reviewing. We had to have something more positive to sell.

Meantime on the island things were deceptively quiet, apart from the raging press battles. The sabotage campaign had not yet begun. Foreign diplomats were being sent to Nicosia on short visits to survey the situation at first hand before the United Nations debates began. I recall taking a Canadian diplomat on a tour of the environs of Nicosia on a Saturday afternoon. He had just remarked that 'everything seems very quiet here' when a brick came through the back window of our car. A large crowd was emerging from a local football match as we passed and the sight of a car with a government number plate was enough to make us a target. I have rarely seen a diplomat revise his considered opinion more rapidly.

Meantime at the UN in New York, where the Greeks imagined that everything else would stop to deal with Cyprus, the usual manoeuvring over the agenda was going on. Various cross-currents of opinion were surfacing and much lobbying was under way. The preliminary vote in the General Committee for admitting the Greek item onto the agenda was passed by nine votes to two with three abstentions. This was confirmed in the Plenary meeting next day, despite an effort by Dr Jamali of Iraq, who later became a close friend of mine, to get the vote postponed to permit more direct talks between the British and Greek delegations: the vote was 30 for the motion, 19 against with 11 abstentions.

However, to the disappointment of the Greeks, a clause had been inserted deferring action on the Cyprus item till the end of the Committee's agenda. The result was that discussion only began on 14th December when the New Zealand representative introduced a motion saying that 'for the time being it does not appear appropriate to adopt a resolution on the question of Cyprus'. The Greek representative naturally opposed this, but on 17th December the Assembly accepted the New Zealand proposal by 50 votes to none, with eight abstentions. This outcome, which was obviously a disappointment to the Greeks, reflected the sensitivity of a great many countries to anything involving changes in frontiers or anything that seemed like outside interference – for example, by neighbours – in their domestic affairs. *Enosis* had also proved a more difficult idea to sell than straightforward independence. On the other hand, the Cyprus question had been accepted onto the agenda of the United Nations and there it remains today, as unfinished business almost 50 years later, despite the granting of independence to the Republic of Cyprus in 1960.

With the close of the General Assembly I was recalled to London and started work on an entirely new job. It seemed as if my brief connection with Cyprus had come to an end. It had been short, mostly pleasant, and I had made valued friendships in both the Greek and Turkish communities. When I arrived I had had a sense that the colonial administrators, however efficient, were leading rather cocooned lives, and I therefore resolved to widen my own circle of acquaintances as much as I legitimately could. One such acquaintance who became a permanent friend was Ploutis Zervas, a well-known Marxist. His story was an unusual one. In 1925 he and two other young Greek Cypriots had been spotted by some unknown agent and removed to Moscow. The other two had disappeared in the periodic purges which plagued the Soviet Union in the 1930s. Zervas, however, had been despatched to Greece on Communist party duties, and so had survived. He remained in Greece until after the Second World War when he returned to Cyprus, with his wife and two sons, in a much more sub-dued and thoughtful frame of mind. He played a relatively small role in Cyprus thereafter, but I found him an engag-ing personality and an unexpected source of information on what was really going on in the island. I last saw him in the 1980s when he was living alone in modest circumstances in the outskirts of Nicosia. One side of his small sitting-room was occupied by an impressive collection of the works of Marx and Lenin, all splendidly bound, while the other wall was dominated by a striking modern painting of Jesus Christ – perhaps a comment on the battle of allegiances still going on in Zervas's life.

But despite my return to London, my links with Cyprus were shortly to be reactivated in a wholly unexpected way.

My brother Ken was then working as a journalist on *The Times* in London. Early in 1955 he was informed by his Foreign Editor that the Cypriot proprietor of the English-language paper *The Cyprus Mail* had turned up in London seeking the help of *The Times* in finding a new editor. After interviews the job was offered to my brother, and suddenly I was again involved in Cypriot affairs from quite a new angle.

My brother flew out to Nicosia as the sabotage cam-paign of Eoka was increasing and took up residence in Ledra Street in order to be near his editorial office and the printing press. Ledra Street later became known as 'the murder mile' because many British, both civilians and mil-itary, were gunned down there, but Ken survived unscathed. Moreover, as world interest grew in the Cyprus emergency, he found himself not only producing *The Cyprus Mail* seven days a week in hazardous conditions but also filing stories simultaneously to *The Times*, the BBC, *The Observer* and *The Evening Standard*. It was hair-raising work but he greatly enjoyed it and gradually acquired an international reputation as an authority on Cypriot and East Mediterranean affairs. He became what is often called 'a seasoned foreign correspondent' and served not only in Greece and Turkey but in such hot-spots as the Congo, Vietnam and Azerbaijan. He also worked for *The Economist* magazine in London for several years as editor of their Foreign Report, but in the end he retired to Cyprus and eventually died in Nicosia in April 1994.

As Ken watched the Cyprus emergency grow from his perilous vantage-point in Ledra Street, he felt driven one night to put a phonecall through to our mutual friend Peter Howard in England. Peter Howard had been one of Fleet Street's best-known journalists but by 1955 had become one of the leaders of Moral Re-Armament. Ken's late-night message was: 'The situation here is getting desperate. If there is anything can do to help a return to sanity, for God's sake think about it now.'

Peter Howard was married to a Greek, Doris Metaxa, who had been a women's doubles champion at Wimbledon in 1932, and they both took Ken's call to heart. Their first thought was to organise a lunch at the MRA headquarters in London for a number of their friends who had links, direct or indirect, with Cyprus. Amongst those who came were a senior diplomat from the Greek Embassy in London, Sir Hamilton Kerr, Conservative MP for Cambridge and Parliamentary Private Secretary to Harold Macmillan, and John McGovern, Glasgow Labour MP who had earlier had a fiery reputation as a Red Clydesider.

Peter and Doë Howard spoke from their hearts about

their concern over British and Greek friction and the crisis in Cyprus. Without claiming to have any ready-made solution, they invited all present at the lunch to reflect in silence on any constructive moves that could be made. It was in that time of silence that Hamilton Kerr realised that he had himself been governed by prejudice in his attitude to Greece and that he should talk to Harold Macmillan about the need to explore new paths.

After the lunch Hamilton Kerr and John McGovern, with both of whom I remained in close contact, continued their efforts quietly in official circles to bring a spirit of *rapprochement* into the deadlocked crisis. They, and others in MRA, also kept close contact with Zenon Rossides, the unofficial Greek-Cypriot representative in London who had grown frustrated because of his inability to enter into official relations with the British Government. Gradually Rossides' acrimony subsided and, through Hamilton Kerr's initiative, a way was found for him to have a private session with Prime Minister Macmillan at a critical juncture in the complex Cyprus negotiations. It was so secret that he was ushered into 10 Downing Street by the back door. I came to know Rossides well in the 1970s when I returned to the United Nations and he was still serving there as Cypriot Ambassador, and there was no doubt in his mind that MRA had played a helpful part along the road towards Cypriot independence.

The lunch arranged by the Howards started a long-running association of Moral Re-Armament with the affairs of Cyprus. A Swiss couple, Marcel and Théri Grandy, who gave all their time to MRA, took up residence on the island and remained there for over 30 years. They built up relations of trust with people in all walks of life, both Greeks and Turks, including many of the political leaders, and left an indelible mark.

No one could claim that MRA or any other agency has

yet found a real solution to the problems of Cyprus. However, when I go out to tend my brother's grave in the British Cemetery in the centre of Nicosia, I often think that when the full story is known it will be recognised that MRA activities in relation to the problem have been a very good example of what the Americans call 'Track Two Diplomacy', the quiet efforts of unofficial bodies to assist, and prepare the way for, more formal diplomacy further down the road.

Cyprus was my first exposure to a phenomenon that has become all too common in subsequent years – ethnic unrest arising inside a country rather than between countries. Of course, outsiders – including other sovereign states – can get involved, as Greece and Turkey did in Cyprus, but these *internal* disputes became one of the most troublesome features of the late 20th century. They have been multiplying on almost every continent, and there are now even signs of them in my own native country of Scotland, not to mention Northern Ireland.

The sad thing is that these conflicts are growing in areas where two or more ethnic groups have lived alongside each other in relative peace for centuries. Switzerland remains a shining example that this is still possible. India also is a miraculous survivor built out of a patchwork of different castes, religions and races. And in Cyprus the Greek and Turkish residents, Christian and Muslim, had got on together, not perfectly but reasonably well, until the end of the Second World War. Nor was it an enforced co-existence – as in the Soviet Union – dependent on British imperial force.

What changed in Cyprus? And what is responsible for the outbreaks of ethnic conflict in so many places – Yugoslavia, Indonesia, post-Soviet Russia, and Central Africa?

Clearly conditions of life have changed for all of us

since the Second World War. There are more of us: we are more mobile and are bumping into each other more. A pack of wild horses can roam the prairie without doing much harm to each other: but put them in a circus ring and you will have trouble. The war itself also had a disruptive effect on settled ways of life and led to the near collapse in many places of social restraints based on religion or tradition.

Religion could be – should be – the highest uniting factor of all for human beings. Unfortunately, it often becomes the reverse. Instead of being a cohesive social force, it becomes a rallying cry for discontents. Religion in itself may not be the cause of the conflict, but it can be misused by disputants to enflame smouldering differences. And religious leaders, finding their positions of authority eroded by rising materialism, have on occasion misused their creeds and turned them into battle slogans. Cyprus itself has not been immune from that phenomenon.

Our choice of leaders is another key factor in relation to ethnic problems. Yugoslavia has demonstrated that, as we shall see later in this book. Although they were both Communists, no two leaders could have been more different in their styles and techniques of leadership than Tito and Milošević. Tito's appeal to the different nationalities making up his country was to forget their past, and by and large Yugoslavia advanced during his rule. Milošević's appeal was to revive Serb memories of ancient wrongs and reawaken a narrow nationalism. It ended in disaster.

The United Nations, because its charter drastically restricts the possibility of action in relation to domestic matters, finds great difficulty in handling such fissiparous tendencies. It is ironic, to say the least, that at the time when the world is shrinking into a global village, there should be more people becoming more passionate about smaller and smaller things. Moreover, an age that has become extremely tolerant on some things, for example, sexual behaviour, has also paradoxically become extremely intolerant of others, for example, ethnic differences.

There may, in fact, be no perfect antibiotic to rid us of ethnic fevers. Safety may lie rather in a realisation that we all have multiple loyalties and we all contain contrary genes in our make-up. Even the Mackenzie clan is known across the Highlands of Scotland for contending reasons. On the one hand, the clan motto is 'Save the King' which is as noble and respectable a goal as anyone could wish. But in parallel there is another much less respectful Gaelic saying: 'You'd better beware of the Mackenzies as long as their bellies are empty.'

Perhaps therefore the road to salvation lies in cultivating balance and equilibrium, and the greatest danger is in becoming what the British writer Bernard Levin memorably called a 'sif', a single issue fanatic.

8

Paris – the linkage of global and intimate

In 1957 I was transferred from the Foreign Office to work with the Organisation for European Economic Co-operation in Paris. To have the chance to live and work in Paris is a privilege and pleasure at any time, but the particular years I spent there were marked by confusion, indecision and often turmoil both for France and all of Western Europe.

The OEEC, encompassing all the West European countries, had come into existence at the time of the Marshall Plan, America's historic and generous gesture which saved Europe from economic collapse after the Second World War. The OEEC symbolised Europe's response. It was designed to help to implement the provisions of the Marshall Plan and to carry forward the economic reconstruction of Europe. It therefore predated the Common Market and European Community centred in Brussels. In the ten years after 1947 the OEEC had achieved many things in the economic and social sphere for which Europe must be permanently grateful: but by 1958 its initial tasks had been largely accomplished and it was clearly necessary to reorganise its work and help Europe to look outward again.

So the work of reorientation began, in which I was involved, and the OEEC was eventually transformed into

OECD, the Organisation for Economic Co-operation and Development, which still flourishes today. However, at the same time the work of the European Coal and Steel Community started by the Schuman Plan was also developing, and under the brilliant leadership of Jean Monnet, the ground was being prepared for what became the Common Market and the European Community. But the membership, and indeed the inspiration, of the OEEC and the Common Market were quite different and it was inevitable that friction and misunderstandings would ensue. Britain, of course, had – wisely or unwisely – chosen not to participate in the Common Market and so two sets of economic planning organisations were developing, the OEEC largely under British leadership and the Common Market under French and German leadership.

The transformation of OEEC into OECD (which has a wider membership, including overseas countries like USA, Canada, Australia and New Zealand) was arduous work but was accomplished without too much difficulty by 1961. However, in parallel, Britain tried to stimulate the creation of a European Free Trade Area, with a wide European membership which was clearly going to cause friction with the more tightly organised Common Market with only six members (France, Germany, Italy, Holland, Belgium and Luxembourg).

The forum for the negotiations on the British proposal for a European Free Trade Area was the Maudling Committee, so-called after the British Chancellor of the Exchequer, and as they took place at the headquarters of the OECD I became deeply involved. They were never very hopeful negotiations and after several months they foundered completely, and with much acrimony, because of the total French opposition to what they regarded as a rival European structure.

During this unhappy period in Britain's relations with

Europe, I was in the pro-European group inside the Foreign Office. I defended British policy as valiantly as I could in negotiations in Paris, but I never felt easy with the views of the highly intelligent individuals who argued that we could afford to 'wait and see' outside the new European structures because 'France and Germany are bound to quarrel'. My view was shaped at least partly by the personal knowledge I had through MRA of Robert Schuman, the former French Foreign Minister and so-called 'Father of Europe'.

By the time I arrived in Paris Schuman had already retired from politics, but it was a moving experience to visit him in his small flat in the Rue de Verneuil in Paris. A bachelor, he lived in the utmost simplicity and there was almost a monkish aura about him. He did not fit at all easily into the normal picture of a professional politician. Yet he, perhaps more than any other single political leader, had set Europe on a new course after the Second World War. At the time of the launching of the Schuman Plan for the European Coal and Steel Community in 1951 he took enormous risks as a cabinet minister in driving forward, sometimes without full governmental approval, his vision of a new Europe based on Franco-German co-operation. If the spirit of Schuman had been retained, or could be revived, in Brussels Europe would have been saved many problems.

Schuman's European policy was an expression of his deep Catholic faith and of his profound reflections on his experiences as someone who came from Lorraine on the Franco-German border. It was easy to see how Schuman had responded so instinctively to Frank Buchman, then still a relatively unknown figure in post-war Europe, when they met in 1948. They were kindred spirits. Within two years, though Schuman spoke little English and Buchman practically no French, the former had agreed to write the foreword to the French edition of the collection of Buchman's speeches. In it he wrote: 'If we were being presented with some new scheme for the public welfare or another theory ... I would remain sceptical. But what Moral Re-Armament brings us is a philosophy of life applied in action ... Democracy and her friends can only be saved by the quality of the men who speak in her name.'

It was directly in response to Schuman's query as to whether Moral Re-Armament could do anything to help France's difficult relations with Morocco that Buchman went there with a small group in 1954. This was one of the starting points of MRA's extensive efforts to improve relations between France and her North African territories – Morocco, Algeria and Tunisia. This continued all through the Fifties and I soon became conscious of it when I arrived in Paris.

As a bachelor diplomat I was fortunate to find quarters in the old family home of the Baroness de Watteville on the edge of the Bois de Boulogne. She and her husband hailed from Alsace and they had suffered much in the war, including the loss of their eldest son. They decided to dedicate their large Paris house as a centre for the work of Moral Re-Armament, and especially for the restoration of friendship between France and Germany. It was in this home that some of the first meetings between senior French and Germans took place after the end of the war. Gradually this work of reconciliation expanded, aided by the MRA conferences in Switzerland which were attended by hundreds of French and Germans every year. When I arrived in Paris I found that the house had been, and still was, the venue of numerous confidential gatherings not only between French and Germans but French and North Africans and French and black African leaders as well.

I recall during my stay one dramatic off-the-record lunch, at the height of the Algerian crisis, between some senior French military leaders and a group of Mau Mau leaders from Kenya whose hatred against the whole white race had been cured through their contacts with MRA in Africa. There may have been no discernible consequences from this particular lunch on events in Algeria, but through many such occasions a new element of healing was slowly coming into play in the shaping of French policy. From what I observed happening in the de Watteville villa, I formed the impression that the contacts between French officialdom and Moral Re-Armament were more numerous and more fruitful than was the case in London at that period. And I was similarly impressed by the calibre of the French activists in MRA who were taking part in these exchanges: people like Robert Carmichael, a senior businessman and head of the European Jute Association; Maurice Mercier, head of the Force Ouvrière trade union organisation; Gabriel Marcel, the Catholic philosopher; and, most outstanding of all, Madame Irène Laure, a leader in the French resistance in Marseilles and in the Socialist Women's Organisation at the end of the war. Both Konrad Adenauer and Robert Schuman recognised the value of Madame Laure's post-war work in building bridges of friendship across the Rhine.

Looking back I realise what a privilege it was to live among such interesting people. I think particularly of my hostess, Baroness Diane de Watteville-Berckheim, and of Madame Irène Laure. They were totally different personalities coming from totally different social backgrounds: yet they were close friends and wholly united on fundamental things. Baroness de Watteville was elegant, vivacious, a superb hostess, maintaining the highest standards of social etiquette, yet an indomitable fighter where issues of right and wrong were involved. Irène Laure was quiet, always soberly dressed, socialistic in outlook, but with such a magnetic personality that I have seen her, on one occasion, hush a United States Congressional committee into rapt silence as she expressed her gratitude for America's war aid and outlined her vision of a new Europe: and on another occasion, captivate a group of German military conscripts in Bonn when speaking on a similar theme. On moral issues, as she had shown during the war, she had the same indomitable spirit as Baroness de Watteville regardless of the consequences for herself.

Robert Carmichael was proud of his Scottish ancestors from Dundee, the early home of the jute industry. He was tall, handsome and charming but the most remarkable thing about him was that, because of his integrity, he was as respected amongst the jute growers in Bengal and East Pakistan as he was in the highest industrial councils of Europe. He constantly walked with a shooting stick but rarely was free from pain, and he was the first person I ever met who had had a hip replacement, then a rare surgical operation.

Gabriel Marcel was another contrasting type. He was a five-star intellectual, and the epitome of the absent-minded professor. I once saw him, during an animated lunch-time conversation, put his food directly onto his place-mat because he had already brushed his plate aside as being irrelevant to the discussion. Philosophically he was the champion of 'Christian existentialism' in opposition to Jean-Paul Sartre. He was an abstract thinker, and his undoubted attachment to Moral Re-Armament, evident in many of his books, always surprised me. He himself explained it by saying that it was MRA's 'linkage of the intimate and the global' which intrigued him.

So life in Paris was proving a most interesting experience for me, both because of my job and because of these extra-curricular experiences. But what made it more enriching – and I would be tempted to say pre-ordained – was that it was during this same period that I met my future wife.

Ruth Hutchison was the daughter of a Scottish businessman and I had known her family through our common association with MRA in Glasgow. Ruth had first gone to France straight from school and had lived with the Carmichael family, learning French and helping the work of MRA. She knew more about the French way of life and spoke better French than I ever did. And although I had never known her well, I now found her working in Baroness de Watteville's home when I arrived. She feels still today, as I do, that it was Providence that brought us together so unexpectedly in Paris.

Our friendship grew naturally and though nothing had been decided when I had to leave Paris for Burma in 1961, a bond had been established. I guess it was separation that brought home to me in the wilds of Burma that I wanted her to become an inseparable part of my life. I can still remember the day in Rangoon when I was driving in my car and the thought crystallised unmistakably in both heart and mind that I must ask Ruth to become my wife. I was so sure I even stopped the car to reflect. We were then 5,000 miles apart and so I decided that I had better wait till I was back in Britain on home-leave before proposing formally. However, when I reached London I discovered to my chagrin that Ruth was in hospital in Switzerland recovering from an appendix operation. So the Mackenzie-Hutchison betrothal took place, to our mutual surprise, in the garden of a hospital in Berne and we were married in London six weeks later – four days before I was due to return to Burma.

My assignment in Paris had been full of unexpected developments. I had been introduced to the challenges of European integration but I had learnt how complicated this process is: in fact, it remains unfinished business even today. I had lived through the political turmoil leading to General de Gaulle's return to power in 1958 and the subsequent ending of the bitter war with Algeria: and I had also seen how a new spirit was beginning to appear in France's relations with her former colonies and protectorates. But most exciting of all, I had the surprise gift of finding in Paris my future partner who was going to enrich my life in the years ahead and without whom a great many things, including probably the writing of this book, would never have happened.

9

Burma – rich country, poor government

Almost exactly ten years after my arrival in Thailand I was
en route back to Asia, this time as Commercial Counsellor
in the Embassy in Rangoon, and my reactions this time to
an Asian posting were rather different. The hesitation was
replaced by anticipation. For one thing I already knew
Burma. While in Bangkok I had visited my friend George
West, the Anglican Bishop of Rangoon, and had been much
impressed by his efforts to build a better understanding
with the Buddhist leadership there. It was the bishop who
established the links between Frank Buchman and the
Burmese leaders who came to London to negotiate with
British Prime Minister Clement Attlee in 1946. I myself had
also tried to encourage the spirit of *rapprochement* between
Bangkok and Rangoon, working from the Thai end.

In addition, I had met some of the Burmese leaders who
had attended the conferences at Caux, including the Prime
Minister U Nu. Indeed the Embassy were not a little surprised when they found that I was greeted at Rangoon airport on arrival by the Speaker of the Burmese Parliament
whom I had got to know at Caux. And I had already a
close friendship with the pioneers of MRA's work in
Burma, two gracious and charming ladies, Daw Nyein
Tha (Ma Mi) and Daw Nu.

And finally, British-Burmese relations seemed in good

shape. The negotiations in London over independence in 1946 with the new Attlee government had gone surprisingly smoothly and Britain's large commercial investments seemed to be mutually beneficial. Moreover, the long-standing commercial links between Scotland and Burma were things I wanted to build on. The Burmah Oil Company was actually a Glasgow-registered company. The Irrawaddy Flotilla Company, which opened up Burma's hinterland to world markets in the 19th century, had long been using shallow-draught boats specially built on the Clyde for use in Burma, and the company's senior officials had traditionally come from Western Scotland.

For my first Christmas in Burma I went up to the silver mine at Namtu, headquarters of Burma Mines, another British company. Namtu is in north-east Burma near the China border. To get there one crosses hundreds of miles of rice paddy fields and then of dense forested jungles until one emerges on a high plateau. The mine is at one end of a valley with steep sides and the smelter is at the other end, perhaps eight miles away, and the ore is carried from the mine to the smelter on a narrow-gauge railway. I inspected the two engines and saw to my amazement the maker's plate: St. Rollox, Glasgow. They had been built for use behind the trenches in France in the First World War and, the war having ended, had been shipped out to Burma where they had been doing 'the smelter run' of eight miles ever since, tended lovingly by a little Scotsman of 5 feet 2 inches, also from Glasgow.

When Jimmy, the engineer, was passing through Rangoon a year later to spend some well-earned leave in Scotland, we noticed that he was taking only one large suitcase. It had a minimum of spare clothing inside and all the rest was crammed with Burmese cheroots. When he returned he said: 'Oh aye, Ah had a grand time,' and taking a cheroot from his breast pocket he added: 'And Ah've still got wan left.'

In fact I never cease to be surprised by the number of links between Scotland and Burma. Walking along the village street of Lochcarron in north-west Scotland, I spotted an unmistakable Burmese Shan bag, with its distinctive yellow weave, hanging on a door. When I remarked to the lady owner of the house that I had recently been working in Burma, a man's voice from within called out: 'And how are things in Prome?' Prome was the centre of the Burmese Forestry Commission where he had spent his entire working life. However great the sins of colonialism, sins of both commission and omission, I have always been touched by the bonds of affection and friendship that obviously remained between the Scots and the Burmese – of all clans and tribes.

Burma has the potential to be a rich and prosperous country. She has been very well endowed with natural resources – silver, tin and copper, abundant forests, jade, sapphire and rubies, oil on land and offshore, fertile soil, and many other riches. The tragedy is that, because of ethnic disputes, chronic insecurity and misgovernment, she has never been able to profit from her natural endowments.

But five months after my arrival in Rangoon my initial expectations were to receive a rude shock, when a surprise *coup d'état* happened in early February 1962. Burma, of course, had hardly known one day of complete peace since independence. Tribal and ethnic loyalties were strong and the roots of federalism still very weak. The assassination in the cabinet room of General Aung San, first prime minister designate, along with several colleagues, soon after independence, had been a severe psychological blow to the whole country almost at the moment of its birth. And in 1960-61 there was considerable malaise and a widespread feeling that U Nu's style of leadership and frequent appeals to Buddhist revival, as a means of underpinning national unity, were ineffective.

U Nu was the most exceptional prime minister I ever met. He had a beatific smile and an air of genuine goodness about him. It was hard to believe that he had any malevolence or cynicism in his make-up. He was in the Gandhian mould. He was a fervent practising Buddhist but displayed no ill will to any other religion. Having been one of the Thirty Comrades around General Aung San, he was identified with Burma's struggle for independence from the start and, when Aung San was assassinated, he succeeded him as prime minister.

He was also familiar with Moral Re-Armament's earliest activities in Burma through his friendship with Bishop George West. Burma's first Foreign Minister, U Tin Tut, who was also tragically assassinated, was another of the earliest Burmese to encourage MRA's activities in South-East Asia. So it was no surprise that later on U Nu should have become the first prime minister anywhere to provide MRA with an official work centre, or 'embassy', in his country.

Despite his other-worldliness, U Nu was a considerable force in international affairs. He was a close friend of the Chinese leader Chou En-lai and negotiated an amicable settlement demarcating the China-Burma border, at a time when Beijing and Delhi were locked in acrimonious dispute over a similar border dispute in the Himalayas.

Because of his friendly personality and negotiating skills, U Nu also played an active part, at the Bandung and Belgrade Conferences, in the formation of the Non-Aligned Movement. He was recognised as a co-founder of the movement with figures such as Chou En-lai, President Nasser, President Tito and Pandit Nehru. The Belgrade Conference in 1961 ended with a marathon all-night session in which U Nu was deeply involved, but in the morning he then drove straight to Belgrade airport in order to come to Switzerland to make a promised visit to the MRA

Assembly at Caux which was then in session. I was in the reception party at Geneva airport and, as he stepped off the plane, I have rarely seen a more exhausted-looking individual. During the hour-and-a-half drive to Caux, high in the Swiss Alps, he scarcely spoke a word. However, as he arrived at Mountain House, a large international chorus in the entrance hall broke into the Burmese National Anthem. It had the effect of an electric shock on U Nu. I have never seen a human being shake off physical exhaustion more dramatically.

Despite their close friendship, or perhaps because of it, the relations between Frank Buchman and U Nu were not confined to mutual admiration. In 1958, when U Nu was making an official visit to the United States, he had insisted that his itinerary should be altered to permit him to fly to Tucson, Arizona, to see Buchman who was recovering from an illness. Notwithstanding the honour that had been done him by this special visitation, which was not lost on the State Department, Buchman went straight to the point with U Nu. He said: 'Prime Minister, you need to learn how to read men – like a page of print.' This unexpected exhortation was provoked by Buchman's concern about the weaknesses, some moral and some ideological, in the people around U Nu.

Buchman's diagnosis proved accurate. U Nu's failure was to match his spiritual quality with realism about the state of his country and the extent of disloyalty and deceit in those close to him. Burma needed not only spiritual exhortation but strong practical leadership, efficient administration and firm decision-making to counteract the centrifugal tendencies that were evident everywhere.

Nevertheless, it came as a complete shock when in the early hours of the morning of 3rd February 1962 the Burmese Army staged their drastic though more or less peaceful coup d'état. They locked up U Nu and other cabinet ministers, seized control of the main radio station and proceeded to put their own officers in charge of all economic operations, large and small. The diplomatic corps (myself included), like the Burmese civilian population, awoke to find themselves under a military dictatorship.

In the British Embassy our first concern was over the consequences for the British companies and banks which had for long dominated large sectors of the economy. We hit on the idea of suggesting that the Rt Hon Malcolm MacDonald, formerly British Commissioner General for South East Asia, and by then British High Commissioner in India, should pay a visit to his close friend General Ne Win, supreme commander of the Burmese Army and chief architect of the coup. This duly happened and Malcolm MacDonald did his best to explain our anxieties. I can still hear General Ne Win's reply in an after-dinner conversation in the Embassy: 'Malcolm, you don't need to get so excited. Just give me two years and everything will be back to normal.'

Things worked out differently. Almost 40 years later, the army is still running Burma and Ne Win, though officially retired, is still Burma's *éminence grise*.

The immediate consequence of the coup for the diplomatic corps was that we found our movements restricted to the vicinity of the capital. Special permission had to be sought for visits beyond a 60 km distance from Rangoon – and the permits were rarely forthcoming. Diplomats were therefore left to decide whether or not to risk unauthorised trips to Mandalay or other parts of the country. I myself flew to the southern port of Mergui, near the Malaysian border, where Britain had long-established commercial interests. But one hour after I had reached my hotel room, a policeman knocked on the door. He informed me that the plane had been detained on the runway and that I should come with him and return to Rangoon immediately.

For other sections of the population conditions were

much harsher. Tens of thousands of Indians and other for-eign nationals, many of them long-term residents of Burma, were summarily ejected. Chinese too were stripped of their wealth and forced to leave. We think of that whenever we look at a camphor chest standing in our home in Scotland, for it was a parting gift from two Chinese brothers – S P and C F Tao, both successful businessmen – who were being compelled to depart, leaving all their material goods behind. Happily, with typical Chinese resourcefulness, they both picked themselves up and went on to amass new for-tunes in Singapore and Hong Kong respectively. Both are still good friends of ours.

Wives of foreigners, including British wives, had rings forcibly removed from their fingers at the airport, on the grounds that the sapphires or rubies were Burmese prop-erty. The meditation room at the airport, a creation of U Nu's, was turned into an X-ray room so that departing passengers could be screened in case they had deliberately swallowed precious stones.

For foreign businessmen the situation was almost worst of all. Their departure would be indefinitely delayed while repeated enquiries were made into their financial dealings. The British businessmen were my special responsibility and it was no easy task to bolster their morale in face of such harassment. Some inevitably fell sick with stress-related illnesses.

The mass of the Burmese people also suffered – except those who could claim family links with Burmese army personnel. Private businessmen automatically became 'the new unemployed' and used to spend seven days a week on the local golf courses. Professional people, Burmese nationals, sought desperately for permission to emigrate. The student population were under permanent suspicion and Rangoon University was periodically closed down because of anti-government demonstrations.

All of this social upheaval was carried out on the pretext of rooting out corruption and in the name of 'the Burmese Way to Socialism', a flimsy document concocted by a shadowy group of left-wing intellectuals attached to the army. In reality Burma's economic life ground to a standstill and the standard of life went steadily downwards until she was classified by the United Nations as belonging to 'the least-developed countries' in the world. The country which had supplied a Secretary-General to the UN – U Thant succeeded Dag Hammarskjöld – and which had once been the biggest rice and tea exporter in Asia, became for years almost a nonentity on the international map.

In such conditions it was extremely difficult, with the best will in the world, to achieve anything constructive. Even the most innocent fraternisation between Burmese and foreigners was suspect, and local people who dared to accept invitations to diplomats' homes had to seek permission and report to the authorities afterwards. The villa which U Nu had donated as a Moral Re-Armament training centre had to be vacated, and it became impossible for any Burmese to participate in MRA conferences in other countries. But friendships which we made in these years continue till today and my admiration for the Burmese who have remained faithful to their principles is unlimited.

As I have explained, during my home leave I had got married and so, despite the unhappy political situation, I had the joy in my last year in Burma of introducing my wife to Burmese ways and to all my Burmese and diplomatic friends. Ruth's appearance on the scene obviously transformed my life. For example, I now had a female intuition to draw on, supplementing and sometimes outpacing my lumbering masculine mind. But for Ruth too both Asian life and diplomatic life were wholly new experiences, and some of her very first impressions had a touch of farce about them.

After our splendid wedding in the Scots Church in Pont Street, London, we had the briefest of honeymoons in Devon and then I had to fly back to Burma because of the demands of my job, leaving Ruth to follow. She thus reached Rangoon towards the end of November which, of course, is a special time for Scots abroad. For it has been my experience that the further the Scots are from home, the more attached they become to the celebration of St Andrew's Day on 30th November. Certainly I have attended more St Andrew's Balls in faraway places than I ever have in Scotland. But in Rangoon, at the moment of Ruth's arrival, the preparations for St Andrew's Day were in crisis. With careful forethought a supply of haggis had been ordered from a well-known maker in Scotland. Unfortunately the strange boxes and the stranger contents had run foul of the suspicious Burmese army personnel who were now controlling the customs at Rangoon airport. The possible effects on the contents in the tropical heat were readily imaginable and so the full resources of Her Majesty's Embassy were called in to help in this national emergency.

I thus found myself – to Ruth's mystification – making frantic trips for discussions at Rangoon airport at odd hours in a desperate bid to save the haggis. This in the end proved too much for my diplomatic skills, and the inevitable happened. But in the process Ruth had been given a very odd impression of the priorities of diplomatic life. I should add, however, that British diplomacy, coupled with the bottomless ingenuity of Hong Kong, triumphed in the end. Very respectable haggis were found in Hong Kong (made by I know not whom). They were rushed to a plane and reached Rangoon, ready for cooking just as the band began to play.

This introduction into diplomatic life was followed very soon by another episode when we were generously offered two geese for use at our Christmas dinner. Ruth blithely set off in her car to bring home the geese, only to find that they were still alive, bound by their feet but still decidedly active. She then arrived home in her small car with her noisy cargo only to discover that our servants, as suddenly devout Buddhists, refused to kill them. Eventually our Hindu gardener did what was necessary.

We lived in a spacious bungalow with its own tennis court where Prime Minister U Nu's son, Maung Aung, was a regular member of our set. We had three servants to look after the house plus a gardener and my driver. They were mostly Indian by extraction. We knew, however, that our cook – quite a creditable performer – came from Bangladesh, but it was somewhat disconcerting to discover that his passport declared his occupation to be 'Docker in Chittagong'.

Underneath the bungalow, which was several steps off the ground, we were solemnly assured by our servants that there lived two cobras. We never saw them once but the servants – and other visitors – insisted that they were there and resisted all suggestions about removing them, much less killing them, as they were believed to be guarantors of good fortune.

The other important member of our household was our dog Topsy. She was an attractive honey-coloured Tibetan terrier, full of amusing idiosyncrasies, and I had inherited her from my German colleague when he was transferred to Stockholm (where sadly he was assassinated by the Baader-Meinhof gang on the Embassy staircase). For us the important thing was that Topsy turned out to be a superb watchdog. Burglaries, especially of diplomatic property, were rife in Rangoon at that time and we were practically the only British Embassy residence to survive intact – thanks to Topsy.

Ruth was at the outset naturally unversed in Embassy

ways. When she was asked by the ambassadress to organise 'a beetle drive' she stared in disbelief – and a little alarm – with thoughts of cockroaches in the bathrooms fresh in her mind. Gradually it emerged that a 'beetle drive' was a card game, akin to bingo, by which Embassy ladies raised money for charities. However, very quickly she learned the ropes and was indeed praised by the ambassadress for the speed with which she took on responsibility in the diplomatic round and accustomed herself to Burmese ways.

In the latter regard Ruth was greatly helped by the close friendship she quickly developed with Daw Nu. Daw Nu, who had worked in Europe for several years with MRA, was a typical Burmese beauty: tall, slim and gracious, with such perfect poise that she could walk, as Burmese women commonly did, with her arms free but balancing goods, such as a rolled umbrella or a bunch of bananas, on the top of her head. I find it moving as I write to think of Daw Nu, now totally blind, still alive in Rangoon in her 100th year, and still faithful to her deepest beliefs.

I, for my part, quickly realised how lucky I was to benefit from Ruth's experience with MRA. Living in homes such as Baroness de Watteville's in Paris and mixing with people of every background in different European countries proved to be a superb preparation for diplomatic life. She had been able to develop her natural gift for languages and in several places was commended for her ability to pick up local accents. In Zagreb, two Yugoslav businessmen approached me one evening at the end of a dinner party and said: 'Excuse us, Mr Mackenzie, but we have been trying to decide: is your wife an English lady who speaks Croat or a Croat lady who speaks English?' She had also acquired wide-ranging culinary skills from her work in Paris and elsewhere, and was secure in the knowledge that she could produce a very acceptable range of dishes at short notice even if our cook went on strike – or returned to the docks!

It was fun doing new things together both in Rangoon and out in the country whenever military permission to travel was obtained. I still think with amusement of our attendance at a very grand state banquet organised by the military government for the Chinese leader Chou En-lai who stopped off in Rangoon on his return from his famous three-month tour around Africa. The evening was memorable for two reasons. It was the first time I had ever had dinner protected by machine-guns which had been positioned at vantage points around the roof of the Presidential Palace, an immense British-built survival of the Victorian era. Several hundred guests dined in the gardens, but whom we were being protected from we were never quite sure. The second memory is of Chou En-lai's speech. It was naturally in Chinese and we all respectfully applauded at the end, only to discover afterwards, through the consecutive translation, that we had been listening to a full-scale attack on imperialism, including the British variety. It seemed too late to stage a walk-out.

Ruth and I were also able to make a fascinating trip up-country to see some of the grandeurs of Burmese scenery and its Buddhist architecture, and in the course of this trip we unexpectedly discovered a little touch of Cheltenham in the jungle. In the hill-station of Kalaw we visited an elderly English lady who lived in a charming bungalow, furnished in best Thirties style, with a luxuriant English-type flower garden all around it. She was the widow of a British Army colonel who had been killed in 1941 when the Japanese strafed an airfield where he was escorting British civilians, his wife included, onto evacuation planes. Mrs Childers opted to stay on and had somehow survived the war with Burmese friends in a detention centre in, I believe, Moulmein. In 1964 she was still in Burma, a gracious survivor of a bygone era, someone who gave the impression of never having consciously harmed another human being in her whole life. To meet such indomitable survivors, especially British women, in faraway places, as we did also in Yugoslavia and Tunisia, was one of the unexpected privileges of diplomatic life.

We enjoyed an afternoon tea with Mrs Childers, complete with cucumber sandwiches, served immaculately by her one Indian retainer. He remained silent throughout but, when I saw him starting to open a carton of cigarettes, I expostulated saying that neither Ruth nor I were smokers. 'Oh, let him be,' whispered Mrs Childers. 'He always does it when we have guests and then he smokes them all afterwards.'

As we left, the retainer suddenly addressed me in curious clipped English. 'And how are things in London nowadays, sir?' he asked.

'Oh, so you know London?' I said in surprise.

'Indeed, sir,' he replied. 'Before the war I was elephant handler in the London Zoo.'

Ruth and I left Burma in 1965 and were not able to return till 1984 when, through the kindness of the British Ambassador at that time, Sir Nicholas Fenn, we were able to make a short visit to see old friends. Virtually our last meal on that occasion was a moving lunch à quatre with Daw Khin Kyi, widow of General Aung San, and Bishop Ah Mya, a successor of Bishop George West, who had undertaken a lengthy and uncomfortable train journey from Upper Burma especially to see my wife and myself. The lunch took place in Daw Khin Kyi's residence which has since featured often on world television screens as the place in which her daughter Aung San Suu Kyi has been detained by the Burmese Army for over 10 years.

10

Yugoslavia – being ready for the unexpected

Our departure from Burma in January 1965 had been under cloudy conditions. This had been not only because of the misfortunes that had overtaken the Burmese people, and also the British commercial community in Burma, but because of the xenophobic outlook of the military dictatorship. It was also because of the sharp reprimand I had received from certain sections of the Foreign Office, and perhaps more precisely the intelligence service, for a private trip I had made to Iran when going on home leave the previous year. Technically, I had erred in not clearing the visit in advance, both with London and the British Embassy in Tehran, but the circumstances were unusual. I had left Rangoon on leave with the intention of spending some days in India seeing friends on my way back to Britain. While there, I was unexpectedly asked by my friend Peter Howard, then one of the world leaders of MRA, to escort Dame Flora MacLeod of MacLeod, my distinguished fellow-countrywoman, and his wife, Doë Howard, on a visit to Tehran, as he himself at the last minute was unable to accompany them. I therefore readjusted my travel plans to make this wholly unpremeditated side-trip to Iran.

We spent about four days there and were most handsomely received by many eminent Iranians, including a number in Court circles, who were friends of MRA or of Dame Flora. During our short stay I did make a courtesy call at the Embassy and informed them of my presence and of our programme. I made no request for help, as all our needs were being met by our Iranian hosts (but not by the Iranian Government). At no time did I engage in any policy discussions with members of the Iranian Government, nor did the Embassy express concern about our visit. It was a private visit to exchange views on the world programmes of MRA principally with Iranians who had already participated in MRA conferences in Europe.

However, when I got back to London, and still more when I returned to Burma after my leave, it was clear that negative – and, I suspect, very inaccurate – reports from official British sources of my visit to Tehran had reached Whitehall and had in turn been relayed back to Rangoon. I was informed that the Foreign Office disapproved of my public associations with MRA and that unless I renounced these associations I could expect no further promotion and it would be preferable if I would resign from the Service.

My own Ambassador, Sir Gordon Whitteridge, was clearly embarrassed at having to be the spokesman of such tidings and made clear that he had no complaints to make about my service in Burma – quite the reverse. I for my part naturally refused to resign or to renounce my links with MRA. I was perfectly at peace in my conscience that I had done absolutely nothing that could have damaged British interests. And so I resumed my duties.

But as my tour of duty in Burma neared its end, it became manifest that the negative stories that had been circulated in London were still having an effect. First one new post was mentioned to me and then mysteriously cancelled. Then the same thing happened a second time. In fact we left Rangoon still not knowing where we would be going next. We therefore had to leave much of our heavy luggage, including most of our wedding presents, in storage. It was only some time after we reached London that I was informed that I should start learning Serbo-Croat and get ready to go to Zagreb as British Consul-General accredited to Croatia and Slovenia.

From a career point of view, Zagreb was not a prize posting. It was then a provincial capital in a Communist country. Neither Ruth nor I had had any previous contacts with Eastern Europe. It was very difficult to visualise what, if anything, one could achieve in such surroundings. And it seemed certain that such a régime would have no sympathy for the beliefs we held.

Moreover, when we arrived on a wet Sunday afternoon everything looked very grey. The sky was grey; the buildings were grey; the clothes were grey and the people looked grey. On our first night I could hear sobs coming from my wife's bed. I asked what was wrong and a tearful voice replied, 'It's all so grey and I don't know anyone.'

This was not too surprising as we had only arrived a few hours earlier, but I think it was a not uncommon reaction on the part of any Westerner posted to that part of Europe in the Sixties. At that moment it would have seemed preposterous if anyone had suggested that we were just about to start a most interesting and rewarding four-year stay in Yugoslavia. In the process we learned to appreciate the unexpected, even when it seemed at first far from favourable. It was the unexpected that often opened doors and made progress possible.

The first very unexpected break in the clouds came less than three weeks later. When I arrived at the Consulate one morning, I found an altercation going on in the outer office between a group of young Africans and members of my staff. I strode onwards to my private room and asked my secretary what was going on. 'Oh,' she said, 'you shouldn't get involved with these people. They are African students and they are always causing problems. Your predecessor said they should never be allowed to go beyond the outer office.'

I could readily see the trouble-potential of this situation, but I had an immediate inner sense that I should get to know more about these men, and I said: 'Well, the next time they turn up, bring them in to see me.' So we discovered their background. They were a group of Commonwealth students, over 20 in number, coming from different African countries. They had failed to get accepted into British universities and had then – *faute de mieux* – accepted Yugoslav Government scholarships to come to Zagreb University. However, they had been given no language training. They arrived with no idea of how cold European winters can be. And they had no embassies or official representatives of their own in Yugoslavia. So they had ended up, very frustrated, at the British consulate.

I listened to their woes, made what suggestions I could, and at my wife's prompting invited them to come up to our house the following Sunday evening. Little did we realise it at the time, but it was going to be good old-fashioned cups of English tea that were going to turn the tide for us. In Yugoslavia in those days Turkish coffee was the commonest, and sometimes the only, drink on offer: but it was very much an acquired taste for an African. A cup of tea spoke of home. Gradually a thaw occurred in our relationships and friendships grew. A few weeks later my wife had the thought to invite them to dinner and to make them jollof rice stew – a recipe which she had learnt from African friends in Paris. This was a favourite dish in West Africa where several of these men came from. The meal was a great success, and we also took the opportunity to show them the film *Freedom* which we had brought with us from London. Originally conceived as a stage play, and written by Africans gathered at Caux, the story of *Freedom* concerned the struggle for independence in an imaginary African country. Much of it was based on the experiences of change which the African authors had discovered in their own lives through their contacts with MRA. The plot showed how civil war in the imaginary country was narrowly avoided through honest apology on the part of the white colonialist and the response on the part of the African nationalist leader. One of Walt Disney's cameramen, Rickard Tegström from Sweden, a brilliant photographer of the natural world, was so captivated by the original play, which he saw on its Scandinavian tour, that he offered to take time out from his other duties and travel to Africa to turn it into a film in 1956.

The film was an immense hit with our African student friends. Some of them had seen it, or heard of it, in their own countries. (President Kenyatta, for example, had encouraged its showing throughout Kenya.) Others thought it would be the ideal film for them to show to their Yugoslav friends in response to the class-war films the Yugoslavs had been showing them. We accordingly lent them the film, and they presented it to Yugoslav audiences in many parts of the country which we could never have reached.

In the following summer some of the Africans wanted to visit their friends in London, despite Yugoslav reluctance to give them their passports to make this possible. On their return they said: 'It's a funny world. Our friends in Britain are all pro-Communist. But we told them they were crazy. They are lucky to be living in a democracy. We're living under Communism and it doesn't work.'

Others of the Africans went to the Caux conference and had their own moral and spiritual roots deepened there. One who went to Caux, an experience which affected his whole life, was a Ghanaian medical student, Ben Markin. On graduating he returned to offer his services to Ghana, only to be refused a job. He therefore came back to Yugoslavia and has spent his entire career there, mostly as a surgeon in Bosnia.

During the civil war there in the 1990s we suddenly heard from him again after a long silence. He said, 'The wounds I am treating up here in the mountains are terrible: but the hatred is even worse. Could I come back to Caux?' By then he was a refugee without travel documents or money. However, we surmounted those hurdles and he visited Caux twice, on the second occasion bringing his wife Hana, a Bosnian-Croat whom we had never met. Then in 1998 came still another unexpected twist in his unusual career: the new Bosnian government suddenly invited him, to his astonishment, to become the first Bosnian ambassador to Japan.

He wrote me from Tokyo on the day he presented his credentials to the Emperor. As he drove in the imperial coach through Tokyo, watching the traffic come to a halt to permit the coach to pass, he said he sat amazed and then reflected, humbly but realistically, that all this was being done 'not for a poor fellow like me' but for the official representative of his newly-independent country. He became profoundly grateful to the MRA community in Tokyo for rallying round to help him to orient himself in his wholly novel situation.

The whole saga of how the Africans in Zagreb grew from being disgruntled and even belligerent students into genuine international bridge-builders did a lot to increase our faith. The story had something almost biblical about it. Certainly the furthest thing from our minds when we were posted to Zagreb was that we should be used there to start off a chain reaction in the lives of African students that is still having repercussions 35 years later.

Although Zagreb, while capital of Croatia, was only a provincial town at that time in the Yugoslav Federal

Republic, it had retained a rich musical tradition from its links with Vienna in the days of the Austro-Hungarian Empire. Moreover, it was Communist government policy to subsidise the arts. We therefore benefited from these twin circumstances by enjoying world-class performances at very low prices. The only snag was the antiquated state of the buildings in which these performances took place. I remember vividly the occasion when Zubin Mehta was the guest conductor at a concert in the Istra Hall, much-loved by senior Zagreb citizens but notorious for its squeaking seats. Mehta had apparently been inadequately briefed about this phenomenon and he stood, facing the orchestra with arms outstretched, waiting for perfect silence to begin the concert. The audience, aware of the dilemma, held their breath and did their best to hold their anatomies motionless, but nothing would eliminate the squeaking of the seats. Poor Zubin Mehta remained standing with out-stretched arms for a considerable time, not best pleased, but finally he had to compromise with reality. Zagreb today, I might add, is the proud possessor of a state-of-the-art concert hall.

Music was also the reason for one of the strangest diplomatic directives I ever received. The British Ambassador in Belgrade, Sir Duncan Wilson, was a great music-lover, and one of his daughters was then studying the cello in Moscow under Mstislav Rostropovich. So when Rostropovich came on a tour of Yugoslavia it was not wholly surprising, although diplomatically delicate, that he opted to stay in the British Embassy residence rather than the Russian. On the day before his Zagreb concert I received a call from Duncan Wilson saying that he was sending his Rolls Royce to Zagreb and that I should – without fail – ensure that Rostropovich got into the Rolls Royce immediately after his concert and drive through the night directly back to Belgrade to have a few hours' rest before giving a recital in the Embassy on the following afternoon.

I assured the Ambassador that his instructions would be carried out and made my dispositions accordingly by getting the Rolls Royce parked right outside the stage door of the Istra Hall. Immediately after the conclusion of the concert, while the ovations were still in progress, I dashed round to the stage door ready to usher a sweating Rostropovich straight into the Rolls Royce. To my consternation, however, I found I had lost my quarry. He had already been spirited away by some enthusiastic members of the Russian colony in Zagreb.

There was nothing for it but to start a tour of the well-known nocturnal watering holes, especially those frequented by Russian refugees. When we eventually found him, Rostropovich was relaxed and happy but not totally responsible for his actions. It was now after midnight and it took the best part of another hour to release him from the embraces of his fellow-countrymen – and women. We then tumbled him into the waiting Rolls Royce, told the driver to lock the doors and not on any account to stop till they had reached the safety of the British Embassy in Belgrade – a four-hour drive. We then phoned the Embassy night-watchman and dropped into our own beds exhausted. Rostropovich's Embassy recital was a success.

Another unexpected gift given to us soon after we arrived in Zagreb was our cook, Rosa. We had inherited from our predecessor another cook who suddenly announced that she wanted to leave but promised to find us a replacement. She produced Rosa, aged 64, who had never worked for foreigners and who was so shy that she almost refused the job. She had, however, been cook to the family of Ban Subašić, the last Governor of Croatia before the Communist take-over. Since then she had lived quietly in Zagreb without taking regular employment. She turned out to be a superb cook by any standards and she and my wife – operating in German and Serbo-Croat – ran the kitchen almost like a mother and daughter. She made us the envy of all other diplomatic establishments in Zagreb. She was also a devout Catholic. She was almost literally a godsend, and when I reminisce in our home on Loch Lomond on the causes for gratitude in my past life, I often think of Rosa.

We lived in considerable comfort in a large Austrian-style villa built on a hill above the centre of Zagreb. It was where the bourgeoisie had lived in the old days, and along our street were similar villas to our own, although mostly in a sad state of disrepair and frequently divided up into smaller flats. Yet inside them one could still find survivors of the old aristocracy living in straitened circumstances but still surrounded by reminders of their former affluence. In one of them we saw a room full of Chagall paintings. The owner, in her eighties and often in her cups, told us that during the war she had befriended a German Jewish actress who had once been the toast of Berlin and who had arrived carrying the Chagalls with her. The city régime who took over the property after the war had allowed the owner to keep the contents (possibly not realising their potential value) on the understanding that they would not be sold and would eventually be inherited by the state. However, in the more relaxed conditions of the 1970s, and possibly through money changing hands under the table, a relative appeared later from South America and the pictures disappeared.

In our own case, shortly before we were due to leave Yugoslavia, an imposing lady appeared at our door and informed my wife that she was the former owner of the house, now living in Ecuador. She announced that she had returned to reclaim her property from the local authorities (and several years later she in fact succeeded). My wife invited her in, and as they talked it became clear that the visitor's other main interest – to the astonishment of my wife – was to know whether 'the treasure in the cellar' was still there. Underneath the house there was indeed a large cellar which contained the ancient central heating boiler. It was dimly lit and at the far end was supported by pit props to counter the risks of subsidence during earth tremors. The cellar was the domain of our handyman who tended the boiler and the grounds of the villa.

The former owner then explained that during the war, when German troops had been billeted in the house, she and her mother had surreptitiously removed large quantities of the family's movable possessions and hidden them in the cellar. Faced with this unexpected news my wife said: 'Well, I have one inventory for everything in the house that belongs to the British Foreign Office, and another inventory for everything that belongs to the city of Zagreb. But I know nothing about the contents of the cellar, so you had better go and look.'

The stylish visitor donned old clothes and, after prowling in semi-darkness at the far end of the cellar, where a false partition with a small aperture had been built, she emerged to announce dramatically: 'It's all there.' My wife wisely said: 'I don't want to know about it. It's not on the official inventories. So you may come back and remove it.' The owner duly returned with a Volkswagen car, and for three days, with considerable difficulty because of the cramped space, she methodically removed blackened piles of dishes, cutlery, candelabras, and the like. She eventually departed but returned two days later and handed a tattered shoe-box to my wife. She said: 'This is for your kindness.' In it we found two charming Nymphenburg china figurines which are still in our home in Scotland today.

Immediately across the road from our house was a modern residence surrounded by a high wall and always closely guarded. It was really the Buckingham Palace of

Croatia, home of Dr Bakarić, Tito's wartime colleague and now head of the Croatian Communist Party. We became good neighbours and in fact Bakarić always referred to us as his *susjedi* (neighbours) and we regularly exchanged token gifts at New Year – in our case some of my wife's home-made fudge, which seemed to be greatly enjoyed. Before leaving Yugoslavia we were invited over for tea. It was a friendly gesture which we much appreciated though the fare was spartan compared with English teas I have known. Mrs Bakarić, herself a professor, explained this by saying: 'You see, our cook is also studying for an engineer's degree in the university.' When we re-crossed the road, Rosa our cook was naturally interested to know how we had got on, but her only comment was: 'Why doesn't she learn just to be a good cook?'

Meantime, with the help of an able staff both in the Consulate and in the British Council, I was reaching out to the leadership and intelligentsia of Croatia and Slovenia, and was finding many more threads of shared experience and common interests than I had expected. I met so many people who claimed to have been present on the night when Randolph Churchill ('Sir Winston's own son', they stressed) had parachuted into Croatia to join the British forces fighting with the Partisans that I was almost persuaded that Randolph must have landed in the middle of a crowded football stadium. In the 1960s these wartime memories were still effective tools for reinvigorating British-Yugoslav co-operation in both the commercial and cultural fields. Repeatedly we discovered reservoirs of gratitude going back to the war years, such as the plastic surgeons in both Slovenia and Croatia who said that professionally they owed everything to the famous British burns expert, Sir Archibald McIndoe, and his team while fighting with British forces in the Adriatic during the Second World War.

Other hidden assets whom we found contributing to British-Yugoslav understanding were the British individuals who had been brought by fate or fortune to Yugoslavia and who had stayed on for the rest of their lives. One such was Fannie Copeland in Ljubljana. The daughter of an Astronomer Royal in Scotland, she had come to Slovenia soon after the First World War to teach English. Her love of the country and its mountains meant that she stayed on as a much-loved English tutor to succeeding generations of local students. Despite her tiny size, she climbed every peak in the Karakoram Alps and became affectionately known as the Gorski Duh, the Spirit of the Hills. When the Second World War arrived, Fannie was arrested by the invading Germans and then removed to internment camp in Italy; but soon after the war ended, she returned to Ljubljana where she eventually died in her 98th year.

Another character from the same mould was Catherine Barić (née Donaldson) whose daughter worked for the British Council in Zagreb. She hailed from Caithness in the far north of Scotland and almost on the very day she had qualified as a nurse in London in 1907, aged 21, she was interviewed and then offered a job in Montenegro by a distinguished personage who turned out to be the Queen of Italy. The Queen's daughter was married to the heir to the throne of Montenegro and, because there had been a number of mysterious deaths amongst members of the Montenegrin royal house, she wanted to safeguard her grandchildren by securing a trustworthy British nursemaid.

Remembering our own visit to Cetinje, the picturesque former Montenegrin capital perched high on the mountains fringing the Adriatic coast, and reachable only via many hairpin bends, we said to Mrs Barić: 'But how did you get up to the capital from the coast in 1907 – by mule?' 'No,' she replied very firmly, 'I went up in the royal Rolls Royce: and what's more, I married the chauffeur.'

She explained that she used to get paid one gold coin per month for her services and, finding nothing to spend them on, she stored them in a belt around her waist. Sadly, when the invading German army reached Montenegro in the First World War, her belt was stripped off her and with it all her worldly wealth. Nevertheless, she stayed on after the war ended, when the independent kingdom of Montenegro was incorporated in the new Yugoslavia. She and her husband later made their way to Zagreb where she brought up a very talented family that is now divided between England and Croatia. My wife and I visited the remote cemetery at the north-east tip of Scotland where her ancestors are buried and paid homage to an indomitable lady.

In 1966 occurred the worst of the unforeseen contingencies which marked our time in Yugoslavia – the Ljubljana air disaster. A British tourist plane approaching the airport at night hit trees and crashed in flames. Ninety-six British tourists were killed, mostly from Yorkshire, and about 20 were badly burned. As British Consul-General I naturally rushed to the scene, and there followed unforgettable days and weeks of sorrow and suffering yet coupled with cherished recollections of a very different sort.

It is part of the normal duty of a consul to offer help to what are called DBSs – Distressed Britished Subjects – who turn up in his or her district. On the day after the plane crash Ruth and I therefore made our way to the Burns Unit in the Ljubljana hospital where the British survivors were being treated. The doctors forewarned us that it would not be a pretty sight. Nor was it. Indeed at one point, as we were trying to convey sympathy and encouragement to a badly-burned Yorkshireman, a fryer in a fish and chip shop in Brough, I felt Ruth tug my arm and she then slid silently onto the floor. The medical staff gathered round and she was placed on a hospital trolley and, before the gaze of the entire ward, was wheeled out into the fresh air. The next day, fully recovered and nothing daunted, she was determined to return to the hospital and, when we reached the Yorkshireman's bed, she enquired how he was feeling. 'Better', he replied and, with a chuckle emerging from behind his bandages, added: 'And how are *you* today?'

There are memories of the fortitude of the British, both the badly injured and the parents and relatives who streamed out from Britain, sometimes only to see their loved ones die. But there are memories too of the unstinted caring of the Slovenes – doctors, hospital staff and the general public. In the overcrowded hospital, Slovene patients were moved out into corridors to make way for the British. When all the emergency medical work had been done, the doctors indicated that the patients could be transported back to England for skin grafting, but the patients themselves decided unanimously that they wanted to stay where they were for further treatment.

When the day for the mass funeral and memorial service in Ljubljana Cathedral arrived, we found every one of the 96 coffins was draped with a Union Jack together with a bunch of wild flowers. The flags had been stitched together by the women of Ljubljana on the model of the only three British flags they could find in the town, and the flowers had been gathered by schoolchildren who had been given time off to pick them. When we commented on the outpouring of care that was being demonstrated, we were told by doctors and members of the public: 'This is our first chance to express gratitude for the help Britain gave us when we were suffering in the war.'

It was good that this sad episode had a positive postscript. The injured British were so grateful for the treatment they received in the Ljubljana hospital that they initiated a fund which enabled doctors from the hospital to go to Britain for short attachments in NHS hospitals. In addition, the Thomson Organisation, to whom the stricken plane had been chartered, made a £20,000 gift available to the Ljubljana hospital to buy medical equipment from Britain, especially for their plastic surgery department. Years later it was touching to meet in Scotland a Yugoslav surgeon lecturing in an international medical conference in Glasgow who informed us that he had started his special research work on microscopes obtained with the Thomson Organisation's gift.

A year later we found ourselves involved in yet another tragic event which revealed a rather different aspect of Yugoslav Communism. On a bright Saturday morning in September we and other members of the consulate were stopped on the Zagreb-Belgrade highway about 30 kilometres south of Zagreb. A long line of stationary vehicles stretched ahead of us and the police informed us that a British bus had crashed further along the road. When I explained that I was the British Consul-General, they took me to the scene of the accident. A bus was lying on its side on the road verge and a mobile hydraulic crane lay nearby. But more horrifying was a row of bodies, 14 in all, stretched out on the roadside. They had all been decapitated by the arm of the crane ripping along the left side of the bus.

I then discovered that the dead were all students from Durham University travelling in a convoy of buses from many British universities who were returning from a Commonwealth Expedition (COMEX) visit to India sponsored by the Duke of Edinburgh. We pieced together what had happened from other shocked members of the expedition, especially from members of the Glasgow bus which was travelling immediately behind the Durham contingent. The driver of the Durham bus, Philip Dobson, being on the reverse side of the bus, had survived unscathed. By him

and other survivors we were told that the bus was travelling northward normally when the mobile crane coming in
the opposite direction unaccountably swerved into their
path.

The driver of the Durham bus was detained by the
police, and the leader of the expedition, Colonel Lionel
Gregory, and one of the leaders of the Glasgow bus chose
to remain with him. The rest of the convoy was allowed to
proceed, leaving behind the dead and injured. Then began
an extraordinary year as the wheels of Yugoslav justice
slowly began to turn.

From the start it seemed to us that the Yugoslav police
and legal authorities were intent on finding the British
driver guilty. They accused him of speeding and of falling
asleep at the wheel. To us, on the other hand, it seemed that
the fact that the bus had stopped for petrol a few miles further back, plus the tyre marks on the road, pointed in
exactly the opposite direction. We believed that the
Yugoslav crane driver must have fallen asleep at his wheel.

The British driver was put up in the home of a Croatian
member of the Consulate staff in Zagreb, and one thing
that convinced us of his innocence was the fact that he
never wavered once in his version of events during all the
cross-questionings and investigations that followed in the
ensuing months. But we sensed from the start that we were
going to have an uphill task in helping him to establish his
innocence. (Incidentally, he later married another of the
Durham students travelling in his bus, whose brother had
been killed in the crash.)

We naturally did everything we could, within the
bounds of law and diplomatic procedure, to help Philip
Dobson. We spoke with all the authorities concerned and
even organised a dinner at our home for local leaders of
the Communist Party to explain to them confidentially the
damage that might be done to British-Yugoslav relations if

the British media, who were showing a lively interest in the case, perceived that Dobson was not getting a fair trial. At our dinner table the Procurator-General, a formidable lady, attempted to argue that the Yugoslavs had the British victims most in mind. She said to my wife: 'We are think-ing of the parents of the dead. They will want revenge and compensation.' Fortunately my wife was able to quote to her from the private letters we had received from many of the bereaved parents explaining their feelings in moving terms and asking that we should do all in our power to get Dobson a fair trial as they thought he had already suffered so much.

However, our efforts were to no avail. When the trial finally came, Philip Dobson was found guilty of manslaughter and given a maximum sentence of seven years in jail. Our consulate staff, including the Yugoslavs, were in tears. Our much-loved cook Rosa said simply: 'It is not the first time in Yugoslavia that an innocent man has been found guilty.'

It remains difficult for me still to fathom what was dominant in the Yugoslavs' minds. Possibly it was fear, fear of large insurance and compensation claims. Possibly it was nationalism. There was never evidence of anti-British sentiment, but there were moments when it seemed that many of the Yugoslavs were in the grip of a logical process which said: 'This accident would not have hap-pened unless the foreigners were here. Therefore the for-eigners must have been wrong.' Possibly, too, the unforgiving characteristics in Marxist philosophy, as evi-denced at our dinner party, played a part.

In any event, the foreseeable outcries in the British media immediately followed and the fact that the trial happened to finish just before the Whitsun holiday week-end, when Parliament and British public life were at a standstill, meant that the tabloids had even less material than usual to turn into headlines. However, when things were at their blackest and Dobson had just been incarcerated, an entirely different set of circumstances came into play. It so happened that the British Foreign Secretary, Michael Stewart, arrived on a long-planned official visit to Yugoslavia. I was immediately summoned to Belgrade and asked to give him in private a wholly honest assessment of the affair. This I did. He said little, but a few days later back in Zagreb, in the midst of our garden party for the Queen's Birthday, I got my first and only telephone call from President Tito's personal office to say that a presidential pardon had been granted to Philip Dobson and he was being released forthwith.

There is little doubt, I think, that the visit of the Foreign Secretary and the accompanying media attention convinced President Tito that a positive gesture was essential at that moment, in the wider interest of British-Yugoslav friendship. I got an unusual personal telegram from the Foreign Secretary, on hearing of Dobson's release, in which he said: 'I am well aware of all the trouble you have taken personally over this case. Well done.'

*   *   *   *   *

In between the dramas of the air crash and the bus crash, we had of course many chances to enjoy brighter sides of Yugoslav life. I recall, for example, that we received invitations to a Zagreb charity ball which announced that 'national dress' could be worn. I was sure that this was an incentive to the Croats, Serbs and Montenegrins to get out their traditional multi-coloured costumes, but I decided to meet the challenge by appearing in my Mackenzie kilt. To my surprise I was awarded a prize for one of the best costumes of the evening, and the satisfaction was heightened by the fact that the prize was presented by a stunning Miss Yugoslavia who had just returned from the finals of the world beauty contest in London. However, the euphoria was short-lived when I found what the prize envelope contained: a one-way ticket to Communist Albania – with which Britain did not then have diplomatic relations!

This is not a book about sight-seeing. Yet no record of our years in Yugoslavia would be complete without recognising at least some of the most striking features of that country and the pleasure we had in visiting such places. The delights of the Adriatic are known to millions and we shall never forget cruising through the bare but beautiful Kornati Islands with Dr Ivo Margan, then Health Minister of Croatia, in the government's medical boat, normally used for transporting patients from the islands to mainland hospitals; nor our visit to Vis, the rocky island in mid-Adriatic where Tito and a few of his closest lieutenants sought refuge in the darkest days of the war, along with British agents fighting with the Partisans.

But it was the most northerly republic of federated Yugoslavia, Slovenia, that yielded the most memorable surprises: climbing Triglav, Yugoslavia's highest mountain (9,400 ft), with Professor Janez Milčinski of Ljubljana University, whom we first met at the scene of the Ljubljana air-crash; strolling through the quiet little village of Lipica which still houses the original stud of the famous white horses, the Lipizzaners, now more often associated with the Spanish Riding School in Vienna; and the unforgettable Skočjan caves with their immense stalactites and rushing underground river heading for the Mediterranean, which brought Coleridge's 'sacred river' in Xanadu vividly to mind.

The south of old Yugoslavia held just as many physical and architectural treasures: the Orthodox monasteries of Serbia and Kosovo, the Shangri-la quality of Cetinje, the ancient capital of Montenegro, and the placid beauty of Lake Ochrid in the hills bordering Albania, with its rare and delicious trout. Nor can we ever forget the old-world beauty of Sarajevo and Mostar (with its 16th century bridge then still intact but tragically later destroyed in the Yugoslav civil war), splendid reminders of the more positive achievements of the Ottoman Empire.

Yet even in the remotest parts of Yugoslavia we rarely felt wholly separated from Britain. On a trip through Kosovo our Rover 2000, one of the first of its marque in the country, suddenly developed dynamo trouble and shuddered to a stop on a bare hillside just before dusk. Providentially, a *Hitne Pomoć*, or first-aid van, appeared from nowhere and towed us ignominiously to the nearest town, Prizren. There in a local garage we found, believe it or not, a young mechanic just back from an engineering course in Newcastle who knew exactly what was needed and had us on our way within 24 hours.

*   *   *   *   *

It is true that we did not deal in Zagreb with the large-scale international problems that were normal, for example, at the United Nations. We did not even deal often with national problems which were the business of the Embassy in Belgrade. But, often in unexpected ways, we found ourselves dealing with issues that gave us a wide range of insights into Yugoslav life.

We were also fortunate in the timing of our sojourn there. The secret police, UDBA, were still active – as we quickly discovered even in our own circle of friends. The notorious Goli Otok prison camp, on a Mediterranean island, was still functioning. People of whom the régime did not approve became non-persons as far as public life was concerned. But by the late Sixties the rigidities of Marxism had worn down. May Day was celebrated by more picnics than ideological parades. At Christmas there were even carols on the loudspeakers in Zagreb's main square, much to the disgust of the Party faithful. Tito himself, whatever his earlier brutalities, had become more of a *grand seigneur* who was received in palaces – both presidential and royal – around the world. And ordinary Yugoslavs were being given passports and felt freer to fraternise with foreigners.

The result was that we could go anywhere (unlike in Burma) and establish friendships even with party officials in a way that had been virtually impossible for my predecessors. We used to visit their *vikendicas* – modest country houses in the hills or on the Adriatic – where they would talk with a frankness unimaginable in government offices. I recall one such weekend with a senior official where we sat on the beach and he reminisced about his life as a Partisan and then a junior party member. 'In those days,' he said, 'we voluntarily gave half our pay to the cause. We don't do that any more!' And then he added, half provocatively and half appealingly: 'Tell me, what do you do with selfish people in the West?'

I felt I could only be honest about the problems we also face, but I was grateful to be able to cite examples where I knew of key individuals in different walks of life who had changed both their behaviour and their whole outlook on life. My friend's interest was obvious and we continued to talk in this vein for two hours, while the Mediterranean glistened invitingly only a few yards away. That talk grew into a deep friendship lasting long after our departure from Zagreb.

The 'year of revolution' in the universities of many Western democracies, 1968, also caused ripples of unrest inside Yugoslavia. The senior official appointed to 'supervise' the students of Zagreb at that time paid a visit to our home to meet my wife's parents. His dilemma, as he frankly admitted, was that he had two daughters who were themselves students. He then began to speak of his own experiences as a teenager with the Partisans during the war.

'We were helping the wounded,' he said. 'One day they brought in a severely injured man whom I recognised as one of my heroes, a man who had fought as a Communist in the Spanish Civil War. Suddenly he opened his eyes and said: "Young man, do you believe in God?" I was shocked and replied: "Of course not, comrade. You know we don't believe in God." Then he looked at me and said simply: "Well, when it comes to dying, you think of these things."' Our friend then looked at us and said: 'As I try to do my job these days, I often wonder if we were right to abolish God before we had something to put in his place.' He too became a lasting friend and later participated in an MRA conference in Switzerland.

There is no doubt that a quest was going on in Yugoslavia in those days for beliefs bigger and deeper than Marxism. To some extent this trend went on in parallel with a rise in local nationalism and a desire for more regional freedom from the rigid controls of Belgrade. As long as Tito remained, these centrifugal tendencies were held in check, but after his death they began to threaten the stability and unity of the whole country with the tragic consequences we all know about.

The danger point was reached when Slobodan Milošević emerged as leader of Serbia and by a series of manoeuvres seized control of Yugoslavia. His whole style and philosophy of leadership was the very opposite of Tito's. Tito's technique, certainly in his more mature years, was to play down the past and get people to concentrate on the future. 'Brotherhood and Unity' were the official slogans. His aim was to make people proud of being Yugoslavs. Yugoslavia became a leader of the Non-Aligned Movement, and a prominent participant in the United Nations. Yugoslav sports teams, especially their footballers, were promoted and encouraged to aim at becoming champions of Europe, if not of the world. In a sense this trend reached its zenith with the triumph of the Winter Olympic Games in 1984 in Sarajevo, in which all Yugoslavia played a part.

Milošević's philosophy was very different. From the start he encouraged people to look backwards. He sought to build a power-base by constantly reminding Serbs of their past glories and of how they had suffered at the hands of their neighbours – Croats, Bosnians, Kosovars, Austro-Hungarians, Germans, etc. It was this mentality which sucked the Yugoslavs into the fratricidal conflicts of the 1990s, including the horrors of Vukovar and Srebrenica and the siege of Sarajevo.

As this conflict worsened and Yugoslavia disintegrated, although I had left the country many years earlier and had since retired, I found myself thinking unexpectedly one morning in 1992: 'Reach out to the Serbs.' All my own past attachments had been to Croatia and Slovenia and I had relatively few contacts in Serbia. However, just at that moment I received a message from a Norwegian friend asking if I would take his place in responding to a request from Milovan Djilas, the rebel Yugoslav leader, to come urgently to Belgrade for consultations in view of the deteriorating situation. My Norwegian friend had been hoping to invite Djilas himself or other Serb leaders to the annual MRA conference at Caux. Although I knew Djilas only slightly, I felt I must go and invited another friend, an English publisher who was married to a Yugoslav, to accompany me.

It was a strange mid-winter journey. As Belgrade was isolated as far as international air traffic was concerned, we flew to Budapest and then continued by a very slow train, with repeated stops and checks by Hungarian and Yugoslav guards, to Belgrade. We stayed at the Metropol Hotel where almost the only other guests were the intrepid aid workers – mainly Scandinavian – who were ferrying in humanitarian supplies over hazardous mountain roads to both sides of the conflict in Bosnia. The other thing that astonished me in the hotel was to notice in the ornate bar that, in all the mural photographs of President Tito with world celebrities which covered the walls, the face of Tito, a Croat by birth, had been defaced. Such was the degree of Serb nationalism.

On the first morning my friend and I went to visit Djilas in the old-style apartment in the centre of the city which he had occupied for many years – when not in prison. Djilas, a Montenegrin, had been one of the chief progenitors of Communist Yugoslavia. For years at Tito's side, he had then become a Balkan Thomas à Becket, speaking out fearlessly against corruption in 'the new class' who were running Yugoslavia and spending many years in prison as a consequence. He now sat before us, completely white-haired but very alert. Whatever the reputation of his ruthless, rabid youth, he had become detached, modest, humorous, mild-mannered and philosophical. He gave us introductions to various people who he thought might be interested in the Caux conference and wrote out for us a message to the conference, spelling out his own vision for Europe. So we started on our round of private calls to people of many backgrounds: Djilas' friends amongst the 'liberals', a Yugoslav diplomatic friend of mine from New York days, two relatives of my travelling companion, university professors and representatives of the Orthodox Church. It was slow work. We were received politely but almost everywhere ran into a barrage of resentment against the outside world. But a start had been made. It was only the first of numerous visits. Gradually we began to develop friendships which enabled us to get under the carapace of Serb nationalism. And today (2001) some of these friends are part of the Kostunica government.

I had served under two very able ambassadors in Yugoslavia in the 1960s, Duncan Wilson and Terence Garvey, both of whom later became ambassadors in Moscow: but neither of them would have believed possible the ethnic bloodbath that accompanied the disintegration of Yugoslavia in the 1990s. Nor did I myself foresee such an outcome of the internal rivalries which we all knew to exist in the Yugoslav Federation. The bloody disintegration of Yugoslavia in the 1990s is such a stain on European history that one is bound to ask oneself why it happened, and whether it need have happened.

Different factors were obviously involved. One was the collapse of the Soviet Union which melted the ideological glacier which had held Europe together in its frozen grip throughout the Cold War. All across Europe currents of water began to flow again, some purifying and healthy; but others poisoned and deadly. Democratic freedoms started to grow again, but so did corruption and hatred. Yugoslavia fell into the second category. To this negative background situation there was added the nationalistic, divisive, ruthless style of leadership adopted by Slobodan Milošević. But in addition there was undoubtedly a failure of leadership in Europe as a whole. Politicians and officials alike failed to grip the situation. They wasted months and years looking for painless solutions which did not exist. Nor did the United States – or the United Nations – give effective leadership either, at least until 1995.

The trouble started in Kosovo when Milošević seized power in 1988 and it ended in Kosovo in 1999, or more accurately when he was removed from power by the determined street demonstrations in Belgrade in October 2000 which were at least in part a result of the Kosovo débâcle. But in between these points, a full-scale tragedy had been played out, act by act, in Vojvodina, Slovenia, Croatia and Bosnia while the international community looked on, confining itself to what it termed 'humanitarian action'. Many of us who had known Yugoslavia earlier tried to get Britain to play a more active part especially at the early stages of the conflict, but Whitehall showed no disposition to draw on the reservoirs of goodwill, dating back to the Second World War, which had been so evident when I was there in the 1960s. Indeed at the time of the Maastricht Conference there were clear signs that Yugoslavia was only a pawn on the European chessboard which could be sacrificed in return for secret deals and bigger gains elsewhere.

There is still no doubt in my mind that the problem could have been handled differently, especially if it had been gripped earlier. As the unsettling implications of the collapse of Communism began to reveal themselves, there was a strong case – which I and others tried to make – for the Western European countries to say not only to Yugoslavia but to all the countries in the area: 'We propose a Standing Balkan Conference to help you through this difficult period. We know you all want closer relations with the European Union and help from Brussels. We warn you that this is out of the question if you resort to physical force to settle your problems. But we promise that we will stand by you, as these problems are dealt with in a Standing Balkan Conference.'

However, such suggestions were rejected, principally for financial reasons. But when it comes to costs, who can compare the probable cost of a Balkan-wide approach with the astronomical expenditure incurred in the subsequent fighting? And we now have a Balkan Stability Pact signed in 1999 which is trying to cope with some of the very issues that were first appearing in 1989. On 28th August 2001 the newly appointed British Foreign Secretary, Jack Straw, acknowledged that 'recent history teaches us that if we do not act early enough, we end up having to do far more later in much more difficult circumstances'. Unfortunately it was almost impossible to get a hearing for such views in Whitehall in 1990-91.

Major efforts are now under way, at both a European and a United Nations level, to strengthen the institutions dealing with such problems and to develop the techniques of what is called 'prevention diplomacy'. But useful though such efforts are, they cannot conceal the truth that the failures dramatised in the mishandling of the Yugoslav crisis were failures of will more than of institutions. They were moral failures more than diplomatic failures.

11

Tunisia – learning Arab ways

From Zagreb we moved – unexpectedly on promotion – to take over the Embassy in Tunis, our first acquaintance with the Arab world. In British diplomatic circles, Tunisia is known as a small country with one of the most beautiful embassy residences in the world. It is built like a Moorish palace on the outskirts of the city and on the fringe of ancient Carthage. It has over 16 acres of gardens around it, including olive and orange groves. It is said to have 34 rooms, although we only found 33. Many of the interior walls are tiled, giving a colourful and cooling effect in hot weather. Several of the ceilings are decorated with delicate Arabic calligraphy carved in the plaster. In one wing there is a nest of small decorative bedrooms which some people believe had been a harem in olden times. The ballroom is dominated by an immense portrait of the young Queen Victoria on horseback, painted by the Count d'Orsay, a remarkable Anglo-French dandy of the 19th century, talented as a horseman, fencer, boxer, and as a sculptor and portrait-painter as well.

The whole property owed a great deal to a resourceful Consul, Sir Richard Wood, who presided there for over 20 years in the middle of the 19th century. Arriving in 1856, he found himself without a residence and had to lodge first of all with the French consul. But sharing a flat was not

Wood's style and he speedily did a deal with the Treasurer of the Bey of Tunis to take over his family residence, the Palais Ben Ayyad, which he then doubled in size, adding a large tiled hall (the ballroom) with loggia and a graceful open staircase. The Bey of Tunis, not London, seems to have financed these extensions, possibly because he was keen to have a dignified British presence to counter-balance French influence, and Britain's right to the whole property in perpetuity was confirmed later.

Wood's local influence was such that he even induced the city fathers of Tunis to route their new local railway, circu-lating around the Bay of Tunis, in such a way that there could be a stopping-place at the far end of his large garden. Called Le Consulat, this enabled him to signal from inside the Residence whenever he wanted a train to stop.

We also had our own windmill in the grounds for pump-ing underground water into a very large tank. This tank, painted light blue, served as a much-loved swimming pool, but its real purpose was to water our acres of cultivated land. From the tank the water flowed down by gravity, and via an intricate system of rivulets, opened and closed by the gardeners' hoes as it passed, until it reached the whole property – olive grove, citrus trees, carrot and artichoke fields. I suspect it was some such system that the Romans used when they cultivated the same land two thousand years ago.

The property was kept by three gardeners through a system of emoluments which I doubt if the accountants in London ever fully understood. In return for keeping the Residence gardens and lawns in order, and in return for providing the ambassador's wife with all the fruit and fresh vegetables she needed, the gardeners were allowed to market the rest of the produce. It was a system that worked very well most of the time, without much money ever changing hands between ourselves and the gardeners.

Occasionally, of course, there was a failure of communication as happened with our first carrot crop. It was the custom in Tunis to transport carrots to market by horse and cart, with the carrots tied in large bundles with palm-tree fronds. So when the head gardener enquired one morning whether he could take some fronds for this purpose, I unhesitatingly said yes. I should not have been so simplistic. When I got home for lunch, I discovered the one beautifully-shaped palm tree which graced the Residence courtyard had been stripped so completely that it looked like a shaving-brush. The carrot crop had sold well, but the palm tree took years to recover its splendour.

On the outside wall of the Residence there is a modest plaque stating that during the Second World War it had served for a time as the headquarters of General Alexander (later Field Marshal Lord Alexander of Tunis) and his staff during the concluding phase of the North African campaign in 1943. Alexander called it 'the best mess we ever had in Africa', though he himself lived in a caravan in the grounds and two thousand troops were in tents in the olive grove. It was Harold Macmillan, then Cabinet Minister Resident in North Africa as part of Churchill's Government, who lived in the house with his staff and organised the military and political conferences in it. He described their brief sojourn there as being almost bucolic, like an English country house party, and the house itself as 'rather like a white Chatsworth'.

It was naturally a joy to entertain in such splendid surroundings and we had a constant stream of visitors during our three years' stay. With them, and through their help, we had fascinating chances to explore the riches of the ancient world that lay all around us. We could even unearth pieces of Roman mosaics as we dug in the Embassy garden. A visit by the head of the British School of Architecture in Italy, John Ward Perkins, initiated us into the excitements of the Roman marble trade. We learned how different types of stone were spotted, cut, polished and shipped from all round the Mediterranean, and were then bought and sold, almost as in a car showroom, in a great emporium outside Rome as the glories of the Imperial City took shape.

We had the chance not only to inspect scores of Roman cities on the ground, but to see them from the air as well. The visit of Winston Churchill, grandson of Britain's wartime Prime Minister, and his family, flying in his one-engined Cessna, gave us opportunities to view Tunisia from very unusual angles. The plane was nominally a four-seater, but by strapping the three young children into what was technically called 'the baggage space', seven of us got on board. I sat in front with the pilot, trying to look as cool as a British diplomat should, while Winston navigated with one hand and took aerial photographs with the other. In this fashion we overflew the splendours of El Djem, the huge Roman Colosseum on the edge of the Sahara, the salt lakes where thousands of flamingos circled below us, and the troglodyte villages of the Berbers in the deep south.

One moment of mixed tension and farce in the Cessna remains with me. Heading for the island of Djerba, we suddenly found ourselves engulfed in a thick heat haze which made navigation by sight quite impossible. Winston therefore took to his radio and began calling for instructions. He started with his plane's call-sign 'GAWBB': 'This is Golf Alpha Whiskey Bravo Bravo. We are heading for Djerba. Are we on course? Grateful for instructions.'

After a silence the radio crackled and a deep French voice – either another pilot or an air-traffic controller – replied: 'We have heard you. Yes, you are on course for Djerba. Good luck, Golf Alpha Whiskey *Brigitte Bardot*!'

Official entertaining also produced a crop of amusing

situations. Each year the Embassy organised a Christmas Fair in aid of local charities. It took place in the Residence grounds and all the outhouses and cellars were put to use. One store-room was equipped with dim coloured lights and transformed into Santa's Grotto. My Head of Chancery – a suitably large ex-RAF pipe-smoking extrovert type – was garbed in red cloak and white whiskers and made a handsome Father Christmas, dispensing gifts to awed youngsters. All went well until his own daughter, aged three, appeared on the scene. When she had been perched on Santa's knee, she stared for a while at the white whiskers and then said: 'You look like Daddy ... You smell like Daddy ... You *are* Daddy.'

Another farcical moment occurred during a British naval visit to Tunis. As well as entertaining the officers, on such occasions we normally turned over the Residence grounds, with the tennis court and the swimming pool, to the other ranks. One day I returned home for lunch and walked up to the swimming pool to see if it was in use. Sure enough, I found two young ratings in swimming trunks sitting at the edge. I identified myself and said I hoped they were having a good time. The reply of one of them betrayed an accent with which I was all too familiar. So I said: 'Where do you come from?'

'From Glasgow,' he replied.

I said: 'So do I. But what part of Glasgow?'

'From Ibrox,' he answered.

'So do I,' I said. 'Which school did you go to?'

'Bellahouston Academy,' he replied.

'So did I,' I exclaimed: but the coincidence was too much for my young visitor.

'Oh my Goad!' he said in his broad Glasgow accent and sought safety beneath the surface of the pool.

We arrived in Tunis just after the worst floods for 500 years had swept over North Africa. Ancient dried-up

President Tito visits the British Pavilion at Zagreb Fair, 1968

Departing for Buckingham Palace as the newly-appointed ambassador to Tunisia, with Ruth.

Tunis 1973 – 'one of the most beautiful British Embassy residences in the world'

President Bourgiba in the Presidential Palace, Carthage, 1973 – 'the father-figure of the nation ... with the skills both as national leader and as peacemaker'

Inspecting the British Army Engineers' well-clearing programme in Southern Tunisia after the floods, 1973 – 'we saw the British Army at its best.'

With Ruth at the embassy in Tunis, 1973

With Col. Gaddafi of Libya (right) and Mohammed Masmoudi, Tunisian
Foreign Minister, Tunis, 1973

With Edward Heath and Deputy Chairman LK Jha in Germany during a meeting of the Brandt Commission. '... there would have been no Brandt Report without Heath.'

Loch Lomond – 'the million dollar view'

water-courses had become raging rivers in an incredibly short time. Many unsuspecting people had lost their lives in them; and simultaneously thousands of Roman artefacts, which had lain buried in the sand for nearly 2,000 years, had been uncovered by the surging waters. We have two such Roman plates, presented to us by the Governor of Sousse, on the walls of our home today.

The floods also disrupted the lives of the Berber nomads and the villagers living on the edge of the Sahara. In particular, the wells on which they depended for survival were blocked, first by the water and then by the shifting sands. An international emergency was declared, and amongst the first to arrive were British Army contingents, especially engineers, from Malta. The British-Tunisian operation was a great success and the Maltese-born soldiers, under their British officers, formed easy bonds of understanding with the local people. The engineers not only cleared the wells but instructed the villagers on how to strengthen the supporting walls against future emergencies. One of my first public duties after arriving was to go to a ceremony in southern Tunisia where the commander of the British troops, Brigadier Paul Ward, was being thanked by the local authorities for the completion of the well-clearing programme. We saw the British Army at its best.

It was also moving to take part in 'battlefield studies' with British Army teams who came out from the United Kingdom with survivors of the North Africa campaign of the Second World War to inspect the terrain over which they had fought. It was often difficult – even for survivors, let alone non-military observers – to visualise exactly how such nondescript desert territory could have been the scene of massive modern battles: and yet deeply touching as survivors of the British 1st and 8th Armies recalled – and relived – particular hand-to-hand engagements in which they had taken part.

The Tunisians have been well called the Viennese of North Africa – because they are so artistic and enjoy life so much – in contrast with the more rigid Algerians who are sometimes called the Prussians of North Africa. Their country is situated at a crossroads of the Mediterranean and one feels that they seem designed even by geography to be bridgebuilders, or at least moderators, between their more formidable neighbours, and even between North Africa and Europe. Indeed many of the young Tunisian nationalists living in exile in Paris before independence were influenced by their contacts with the leaders of Moral Re-Armament in France, Habib Bourguiba amongst them. Mohammed Masmoudi, who later became Foreign Minister, once said that but for MRA there would have been 'war without mercy' between Tunisia and France.

However, by the time we reached Tunis in 1970, President Bourguiba, the very active father-figure of the nation, was already suffering from ill-health, and during our stay Tunisia was not playing a very prominent role on the international scene. She was rather seeking accommodations with her more boisterous neighbours, especially Colonel Gaddafi in Libya. But we were party to one dramatic series of events in 1972 which demonstrated that President Bourguiba's skills as both national leader and peacemaker had not deserted him.

Colonel Gaddafi arrived in Tunis with a large entourage on a professed visit of friendship which began to go wrong from the very beginning. Bourguiba arranged a state banquet for about 300 people in the Presidential Palace in Carthage. All the diplomatic corps and leaders of Tunisian society, with their wives, were ushered to their seats. But there was no sign of the dignitaries at the head table taking their places. Clearly something was going awry and after a wait of over half an hour, a very flustered Chef de Protocol informed the diplomats in whispers that Colonel

Gaddafi had suddenly refused to dine in the company of women. The large assembly, garbed in all their finery, remained at their tables, getting hungrier and more embarrassed by the minute. Finally it was announced that a compromise had been reached: Gaddafi had agreed to enter the banqueting hall provided all the men at the high table sat together at one end and all the women were moved to the other end. The soup then arrived.

The programme of the official visit continued, but Gaddafi was pressing hard behind the scenes to be allowed to speak to the Tunisian masses in a football stadium before he left. This gave rise to intense anxiety in the Tunisian Government who wished at all costs to avoid demonstrations and public uproar. Finally a compromise was again reached, that Gaddafi should address a hand-picked audience in the largest cinema in Tunis. The building was absolutely packed and Gaddafi was warming to his familiar themes of Arab nationalism and the iniquities of the Western powers before, during and after the Second World War. Unknown to him, however, the ailing Bourguiba was following the proceedings on closed circuit television at the Presidential Palace in Carthage. Sensing that the atmosphere was becoming overheated, he called for his Rolls Royce and made his way to the cinema at high speed.

Arriving there, he made a dramatic entrance from the back of the auditorium and made his way towards the platform through the cheering crowds. Gaddafi was, of course, forced to stop; but Bourguiba then sat down and signalled him to continue. When he finally ended, Bourguiba moved towards the podium and then for about 40 minutes, without notes, began to answer Gaddafi's wilder exaggerations point by point. It was done very skilfully, not provocatively but in the tone of an elder statesman speaking to a younger and less experienced guest. A crisis had been averted; half-truths had been exposed; but reasonably friendly relations had been maintained.

Not long after this, the troubles of the outside world suddenly touched us again. We received word from London that three Irishmen were believed to be arriving in Tunis on a gun-running mission for the IRA. With the help of the Tunisian police we quickly discovered that the men in question were already in residence in one of the best hotels in town. They were then observed making contact with a ship which had just arrived from Libya. In due course the cargo of this ship was transferred to another which then left with the Irishmen on board. It was not difficult to track the movements of this second ship westward through the Mediterranean to Gibraltar and beyond. When she entered Irish territorial waters, she was boarded by the Irish navy, who discovered large quantities of Czech-made munitions which had been consigned to Libya and then twice reshipped in Libya and Tunis. The prominent IRA activist, Joe Cahill, and his two colleagues were duly arrested and imprisoned for several years.

But our most enriching, and in the long run the most important, experiences in Tunisia were the insights we gained, as newcomers to that part of the world, into Arab and Muslim thinking. It was not long before we began to sense the gulfs of non-comprehension between the Western and Arab worlds that lay not far beneath the veneer of affability, gulfs of non-comprehension, and even hatred, which burst on an astonished world in Manhattan and Washington 20 years later. It was friendships with well-disposed Arabs that brought home to us the major differences of outlook and reaction. One of these was with Fadhel Jamali, former Iraqi Foreign Minister and Prime Minister, whom I had in fact known since the San Francisco Conference in 1945 when he was one of the signatories of the UN Charter.

During the *coup d'état* in Iraq in 1958, which ended the monarchy and established a dictatorship under General Qasim, Jamali had been arrested and condemned to death. Indeed, news of his execution had been flashed around the world and, when this proved premature, Pope John XXIII, Dag Hammarskjöld and many world leaders had intervened on his behalf. Eventually he was sentenced to 55 years' imprisonment, but after three more years in detention was released by Qasim, who was himself assassinated two years later. After his release, Jamali flew to Switzerland at the invitation of MRA friends and from there to Tunisia where President Bourguiba had generously offered him refuge.

We now refound Jamali teaching in Tunis University and living quietly with his Canadian wife in a small house on the heights outside the city with spectacular views across the Bay of Tunis. He had a hobby of collecting walking sticks on his travels and we used to walk and talk for hours on the cliff paths near Gammarth, covered in springtime with white broom. The Jamalis have had a handicapped son living in a nursing establishment in Scotland for over 50 years and used to visit him every summer. So there was no doubt about their attachment to Britain and to British ways. Yet it was a revelation to discover how deeply hurt Jamali would feel when Britain did something which he interpreted as being insensitive, biased and an expression of *realpolitik*, whatever our high-minded professions. This naturally tended to occur in relation to developments in the Middle East, when Jamali would even be ready to defend the régime which had condemned him to death; but it also occurred over controversial British activity – or inactivity – in the United Nations which Jamali idealistically supported in all weathers. We would often have lively arguments and deep divergences on such issues, but I always learned something from our exchanges and our friendship continued until Jamali died in 1997, and indeed it still continues with his sons.

Apart from Jamali, our mentors in Arab ways were men such as Mohamed Ennaceur, a distinguished Tunisian Cabinet Minister; Sheikh Abdel Rahman al-Bassam, Saudi Arabian Ambassador and Dean of the Diplomatic Corps in Tunis, and Lakhdar al-Brahimi, who later became Algerian Foreign Minister and is still a senior adviser to Kofi Annan, Secretary General of the United Nations. From all of them we learned much about a way of life of which we had been very ignorant. We learned, too, how swiftly a negative reaction can be turned positive when a certain measure of humility and honesty are present. After my retirement I found myself making an after-dinner speech on development matters in London at which Lakhdar al-Brahimi was present as Algerian Ambassador to Britain at that time. In reply to remarks I made about the need for more honesty on the part of Western governments about discriminatory trade and shipping policies in the ongoing debate about a 'new international economic order', Brahimi said: 'I'm normally reluctant to intervene in discussions like this because British speakers on the Third World make me so angry; but tonight, in the light of Mr Mackenzie's admissions, I feel I should say that we in the developing world also need to be more honest about our failures: for example, the gap between rich and poor inside many of our countries is proportionately just as great as the gaps between rich and poor in the outside world, and we need to do something about that.' Within a few minutes an atmosphere had been generated that enabled us to make more progress towards a consensus than was often achieved in UN committees after weeks of discussion.

On our own doorstep in Tunis we had several examples, minor incidents in themselves, of our need to open our eyes wider regarding conventional behaviour in Western-Muslim relations. The first concerned the traditional Embassy Christmas party in the Residence, to which all the staff were invited. It took the form of a glorified cocktail party with carol singing and Christmas trimmings. But it dawned on us that this type of party, although legitimate and good, meant little to our Muslim staff and still less to their families. We therefore planned two Christmas parties in the following year. The British one followed the traditional pattern; but for the Muslim staff we produced Arab food specialities and we made special efforts to make sure that they understood at least something about the occasion we were celebrating. It was a great success with virtually 100 per cent attendance, not only of male staff but of their wives and children as well. I can still see the small Arab children crowded round the towering Christmas tree in the ballroom listening to a simplified version of the Christmas story narrated by my wife.

The other example concerned a poor Arab family of squatters who lived in a hut just beyond our property. We often exchanged hellos with the children when we went out walking. But one day we were shocked to hear from our cook that the eldest daughter of this poor family, aged about twelve, had been killed by a car near the Embassy. We naturally wondered what we could do, and my wife said to our cook: 'Should I take over flowers to the poor mother?'

A look of amazement appeared on the cook's face. 'Why flowers?' he said.

When my wife explained that this was the custom in the West at times of bereavement, he remained perplexed and said: 'But you cannot eat flowers. Why don't we make a big couscous and take that to them? That's what they'll need.'

This brief exchange served literally as an eye-opener. In

an instant we realised the shallowness and inadequacy of our conventional Western approach to the crisis. In the years ahead we often thought back to this event as we grappled with the West's need to give much deeper consideration to the implications of the Rich-Poor gap in the world.

I was involved in another attempt to do something about the hurts of the past which had a less fruitful outcome. When the Tunisian Foreign Minister was making an official visit to Britain, the first such visit since Tunisian independence, the question arose of the customary exchange of governmental gifts to mark the occasion, and I therefore ventured to suggest to London that one symbolic way of expressing goodwill would be to return an ancient stone tablet from the Roman remains at Dougga which has resided in the British Museum for over a century. The special interest of this tablet for archaeologists lies in the inscription which is not in Latin but Phoenician, a reminder of Carthage, the rival colonising power of North Africa. The fact that the Romans so ruthlessly destroyed Carthaginian culture gives this surviving tablet special significance. In Dougga today, which is visited every year by tens of thousands of tourists from all parts of the world, the official guides regularly point to the gap where the tablet used to stand and recite the story of how it was 'stolen' by a British naval captain in the 19th century and now rests in the British Museum in London. I therefore thought that by handing back the tablet to the Foreign Minister we would at once give pleasure to the Tunisians and simultaneously eliminate an item of anti-British propaganda that was reaching thousands of people every year.

I admit I was disappointed when the British Museum firmly rejected my suggestion as inappropriate, if not unpatriotic. I was aware, of course, that there are legitimate differences of view about the retention of foreign antiquities in Western museums. It can indeed be argued that objects such as the Punic tablet are better preserved today than they would be if they had been exposed to the desert storms of Dougga. It can also be claimed that such objects reach larger audiences when housed in famous museums, instead of being left in faraway places, and in this way contribute more to international culture.

But I knew too that, while I was in Burma, Lord Louis Mountbatten had brought back the Mandalay Regalia, which had been removed from the royal palace by British military personnel in the nineteenth century. He presented it to the Burmese Government as a gesture of good will. So such actions can and do happen, and I believe that the pros and cons of retaining such relics need to be weighed carefully in the light of changing circumstances. I felt that the first visit to Britain by a Tunisian Foreign Minister was such an occasion, and I had also at the back of my mind the unusual circumstances surrounding our free tenure of the British Embassy Residence in Tunis for over 100 years.

I was strengthened in this perhaps debatable view when I discovered on my next visit to London that the tablet is not in fact seen by anyone except the British Museum staff. It is kept in a store with countless other objects because there is no room for it in the display rooms. I may be naive, but that also seemed to me to point in the direction of at least a fresh look at past policy.

12

Challenges of World Development – the UN and Brandt Commission

Early in 1973 the director of personnel in the Foreign Office wrote in a helpful way asking what I would like to do for my remaining three years before retirement. He said I could stay on in Tunis, or I could go back to Burma as Ambassador, or I could go to the United Nations as British Representative on the Economic and Social Council.

It would have been easy and pleasant to stay on in our splendid residence in Tunis. We also felt a tug to return to see our friends in Burma and renew our acquaintance with the colourful Asian way of life. But against that was a consciousness that the military régime in Rangoon were as deeply entrenched as ever, despite General Ne Win's assurances to Malcolm MacDonald, and that there was very little scope for constructive diplomacy of any kind (as subsequent events bore out). We therefore settled for the third option and prepared to move to New York where my diplomatic career had begun 30 years previously.

The shock of the transition from our semi-rural existence in Tunis to the noise and bustle of Manhattan was considerable. We found ourselves living in an elegant duplex apartment on Park Avenue. A former mayor of New York lived below us and the daughter of President Truman, Margaret Truman Daniels, was another neighbour. But the sense of rush and non-stop action was almost overpowering. The traffic on Park Avenue never ceased. Even on the 11th floor we were constantly aware of it, and across the road was the Lennox Hill Hospital where the noisy movement of oxygen cylinders and other medical supplies went on all night. We often thought nostalgically of the peaceful quarters we had enjoyed over the previous years in Rangoon, Zagreb and Tunis. However, in due course we were able to move to another apartment where the bedrooms were at the rear of the building, and therefore much quieter, and life became easier.

The transition was initially more difficult for my wife than for me, for she had never lived in New York before. However, she soon felt the benefit of the warm-hearted hospitality offered by the New Yorkers and by our UN colleagues. Indeed, her very newness to New York society occasionally had serendipitous consequences. One evening we were at a glamorous dinner party given by one of Manhattan's top hostesses, and my wife found herself seated between two men whom she did not know. Yet it was obvious that they were both prominent New Yorkers and she quickly sensed that one was from the musical world. Chancing her luck, she asked if the Metropolitan Opera was still as good as it had been under Rudolf Bing, the illustrious English director who had recently retired.

'Mrs Mackenzie,' replied her neighbour, 'you have just stepped on a banana skin. I am Rudolf Bing's successor.' Yet this faux pas started an acquaintance which resulted in our being repeatedly invited to the director's box at the Met during our three years in New York – even to a never-to-be-forgotten seven-hour performance of *The Twilight of the Gods*!

For me the move to New York was much easier, and I quickly plunged into the excitements of my new job in surroundings that I was already quite familiar with. The Economic and Social Council had always been the plain sister to the more glamorous Security Council in the UN family. The Charter as conceived at San Francisco gave the Security Council much more power to make decisions while the ECOSOC is confined to making recommendations. Moreover, the multiplication of UN Specialised Agencies had inevitably dispersed power and influence away from ECOSOC. However, just about the time of our move to New York, two world developments occurred which brought the economic activities of the United Nations back to centre stage: the oil price explosion in 1973-74, which threw the whole world economy into crisis, and the sudden increase in public consciousness of the difficulties facing developing countries, partly as a result of a series of natural disasters plus the increased power of television. The fact that these two major developments, which were not causally related, came together in time produced seismic shudders in the United Nations.

Suddenly there was a disturbing new alignment of forces in the organisation, disturbing at least to the Western powers. In the early years the Western powers had almost always been able to rely on comfortable majorities on issues before the General Assembly. This was thanks to the United States' strong influence over the Latin American vote, London's influence over the white Commonwealth, and Western Europe's solidarity because of the Russian danger. This still remained largely true even after the explosion of membership, especially of African countries, in the 1950s and 60s.

Now, however, all was changed. The 13 oil-producing countries, whose action was the immediate cause of the world crisis, were certainly not poor countries: and the poor countries – over 100, making up the so-called Third World – were suffering from the oil price explosion just as much as the Western democracies were. Nevertheless, the poor countries chose to join forces with the oil producers against the West, and they formed a joint programme for a New International Economic Order encompassing demands for more development aid, reforms of world trade policies, limitations on the action of multinational corporations, reorganisation of the World Bank and IMF, etc. Moreover, the Communist bloc, although they had absolutely no kinship with the oil producers and were giving relatively little help to the Third World, were only too happy to join this campaign for a new international economic order as a means of embarrassing and weakening the Western powers. Thus the Western countries found themselves facing defeats of over 100 votes to 20 on important issues.

The predicament was brought home to me during the discussions of a Third World resolution promoting 'permanent sovereignty over natural resources'. This was, of course, directed against the multinational companies and the Western countries from which they came. But it placed a country such as Britain in a dilemma, for we were desperately keen to defend our own sovereignty over the natural resources of oil and gas under the North Sea. In this awkward situation London authorised me to support the resolution provided five words were added, indicating that changes in sovereignty would only be made 'in accordance with international law'. London felt that this would safeguard our position and they supplied me with supporting legal arguments. I accordingly went to the rostrum and presented our brief amendment as persuasively as I could. When I finished, the Algerian delegate asked for the floor. His intervention could also be summed up in five words: 'But who made the law?' He then went on to explain that what we termed 'international law' was built up from case law going back to the 18th century and earlier, long before most of the developing countries had come into existence.

It therefore reflected the interests of the older countries more than the interests of the new. I lost the vote, as I remember, by 108 votes to 13.

Of course the published programme for a new international economic order was not nearly as strong as it seemed. It was largely a list of demands for change on the part of the developed countries. It said very little about what reciprocal changes developing countries would accept. Moreover, it said nothing about the oil price explosion simply because the poor countries and the oil producing countries had not reached any agreement on that issue. It also was silent on the failure of the developing countries to grow enough food to feed themselves and on the embarrassing question of corruption. Nevertheless, it threw the Western countries completely onto the defensive, especially as we had failed to offer any alternative proposals of our own.

Therefore the Sixth Special Session of the General Assembly that was called to deal with the oil crisis was doomed from the start. The Western countries wanted to talk about the oil crisis and if possible nothing else. The Third World coalition wanted to talk about everything except the oil price explosion. It was truly a *dialogue des sourds* and ended in acrimony and mutual recrimination. A Declaration of a New International Economic Order was passed overwhelmingly, but Western countries – including Britain and the United States – immediately registered reservations indicating that they had no intention of being bound by it.

It was obvious that another attempt would have to be made to deal with all the unsolved problems and unfinished business of the Sixth Special Session. For Britain this presented acute dilemmas. Not only had we ended up on the losing side, but we had got separated from a majority of the Commonwealth, and a Commonwealth Summit

Conference was due shortly. I personally felt that we had failed both morally and politically and that a fundamental rethink of our position was needed before the next Special Session. So this started a year of very hard work on both sides of the Atlantic to develop new ideas and a new strategy. This campaign had to go on first in our own ranks and then with our allies to find more common positions in time. I was fortunate in having Ivor Richard as head of mission in New York, plus an excellent staff to help in this work, and we also had some strong allies at the top level in Whitehall, notably Sir Donald Maitland, formerly Ambassador to the United Nations and by then a senior adviser to Foreign Secretary James Callaghan. We used every channel open to us to move the argument forward with other friendly countries as well, not least the United States.

I sensed half way through the year that a key moment would be the opening meeting of the Preparatory Commission that had been set up to clear the ground for the forthcoming Seventh Special Session. My staff in New York served me up a first-rate draft of an opening speech, reflecting the ideas we had all been working on. I can well remember working on it during my habitual time of meditation in the early morning. The challenge was to find out how to strike a sufficiently positive note, within the limits of my instructions, to convince other delegates and especially those from developing countries that we had something new to say. In addition, there was the background question of whether I should submit back to Whitehall a complete draft of all I wanted to say, knowing well the risk that it might be watered down – if not thrown out – in the process. It was a borderline case, but in the end I felt that I should take the risk of going ahead without formal clearance. I was lucky at that moment to spot in the press a report of a speech that the Prime Minister, Harold Wilson, had made to a women's conference in Oldham in Lancashire, in which he had referred positively to the need to reach out with more help for the afflicted in the Third World. So I used this unexpected item as an opening for my speech.

United Nations committees tend to be rather blasé bodies, but that afternoon something happened. It was clear that I had caught the attention of all the groups involved and the reaction afterwards showed that many of the delegates had sensed that we were trying to bring something new, a more cooperative approach, into the discussions. One particular phrase in the speech about the need for all of us to be ready to 'cross the philosophical bridge of change' caught people's attention and was often quoted in the subsequent months. It set a new tone in the Preparatory Commission.

Of course, that speech was only one single element in a complex process in which many other people and other countries played a part; but the upshot was that the Seventh Special Session of the General Assembly turned out to be totally different from the previous year's effort. Unanimity was achieved about the way ahead with only a minimum of reservations. The Dutch delegate, Jan Pronk, summed up this change by saying: 'This time we talked with each other, not at each other.'

Later the British Foreign Secretary, James Callaghan, welcomed the outcome of the Assembly in a report to the House of Commons and said: 'Our next task is to put flesh on the bones of our new undertakings. We, the developed world, have a duty to make practical realities out of our New York commitments.'

On re-reading these words more than 25 years later, one cannot fail to be struck by the slow rate of progress which has been made in solving the problems identified at the Seventh Special Session and in fulfilling our promises then.

The efforts to resolve the problems have continued in many different international institutions, but progress has been unimpressive. Nevertheless, looking back I feel gratified to have played a part in United Nations events in 1975 and in turning the organisation away from the disasters which were looming in the previous year.

When things go wrong, the United Nations is often the handiest whipping-boy available. Its failures are undeniable. It is slow, inefficient, bureaucratic, and selective in its condemnations. Yet its critics often include people who would never dream of giving it the power to do what they accuse it of failing to do. It is, after all, only an international organisation, not a supra-national organisation, much less a world government. As Lord Caradon, one of its most distinguished British champions, once said: 'There is nothing wrong with the United Nations – except its members.' And Winston Churchill's observation is also relevant: 'The United Nations was set up not to get us to heaven but to save us from hell.'

If it did not exist, it would have to be invented. And if we allowed it to collapse, we should find it a Herculean effort to rebuild it.

The United Nations had been part of my professional life, directly or indirectly, almost continuously since I entered diplomacy. So a few weeks after the end of the Seventh Special Session it was undeniably pleasant to have been an actor in a wholly unexpected little drama in the Economic and Social Council. At the end of the morning's business on 17th October, 1975, the Yugoslav delegate intervened – by prior agreement with the President and other members of the Council – and to my total surprise made a moving tribute to the work I had done in the previous three years, going so far as to say: 'With him arrived a new spirit and a new attitude of his country towards ECOSOC and the solving of international economic problems.' The American delegate told me privately that he believed it was only the second time in the Council's history that anything like that had happened.

*   *   *   *   *

Thus ended my formal association with the United Nations and, as I thought, my professional career as a diplomat; and it became urgently necessary for my wife and myself to consider where we were going to spend the next phase in our lives. We had no residence of our own and most of my Foreign Office colleagues clearly expected us to settle in or near London, apparently on the assumption that culture, if not civilisation, starts to thin out after you pass Watford Junction, or at the most Stratford-upon-Avon. 'Further north' was reserved for holidays or special visits. However, my wife and I, both being Scottish, had a wish to return to our roots. We not only had family responsibilities to think of but felt a desire, having spent most of our working lives abroad, to breathe Scottish air again and to try, if we could, to contribute something to our native land.

This pointed us towards the West of Scotland where we had both grown up, but when we told property agents in Glasgow what we were looking for in the Loch Lomond area and what our limited resources were, we were met with dubious stares: 'Yes, you and 1,000 others.' It was only on the day before we were due to return to my post at the United Nations that we heard through a banker friend of a cottage which was unexpectedly coming onto the market on the eastern shore. We rushed out to see it, liked it very much and made an offer, but then had to fly off immediately to New York, leaving all the negotiations in the hands of our banker friend, Iain Campbell.

Silence ensued and we assumed we had been unsuccessful, but months later we learned about an unusual sequence of events. After much telephone discussion, the owner had phoned our banker friend to say that the bidding was down to ourselves and one other person and she felt in a quandary as to what to do. Greatly daring, our friend (who had never met the owner in person) had replied: 'Well, Mrs Taylor, I am sure there is a right solution to your dilemma. Why don't you pray about it?' The next day the owner had phoned again saying: 'I did what you suggested, Mr Campbell, and I feel the Mackenzies should have the house.' So it was with a sense of gratitude, and almost of awe, that we packed our bags in New York and prepared to restart life in Scotland.

The cottage in which we live beside Loch Lomond is only 27 miles from Glasgow airport and yet is technically in the Highlands. This is because it is situated just two miles north of a geological phenomenon, called the Highland Fault, running right across Scotland and separating the Lowlands and the Highlands.

It is an old stone building with very thick walls built perhaps 200 years ago, doubtless as a crofter's dwelling. It has no architectural distinction and we have had to add three rooms to it. It was one of the builders who dubbed it 'the house with the million dollar view'. We have a right of way to the beach and to our mooring. We have a deer fence to protect the garden, for we quickly discovered that deer treat rose-buds as humans treat chocolates. We have log-fires supplemented by background electricity for the winter months, but we have never been snowed in, as Loch Lomond is almost at sea-level. Our nearest neighbours are half a mile away; and here we live comfortably, surrounded by possessions, large and small, which remind us of places and people around the world who have meant much to us.

It would be easy in such surroundings just to sit and let the world go by. However, two years later, when we were visiting Southern Africa, I received a telegram from a British MP, Robert Rhodes James, whom I had known in New York. He said that Edward Heath, the former Prime Minister, was looking for an assistant in his new job as a member of the Brandt Commission and that, in the light of my work at the United Nations, he had put my name forward.

The full name of the Brandt Commission was the Independent Commission on International Development Issues. The Commission was set up at the suggestion of Robert McNamara, President of the World Bank, and other international leaders as a means of accelerating progress on development issues which were being pursued in numerous international forums following the Seventh Special Session in New York. Its members were to be world leaders from widely different backgrounds, serving under the leadership of ex-Chancellor Willy Brandt of West Germany. It was hoped that because they would be serving in an independent capacity, freed from government restrictions, they might produce new ideas for bridging the Rich-Poor gap.

When I returned to Britain from Africa, I immediately went to visit Edward Heath in his London home. He explained to me what was involved, and I in turn told him of my deep interest in development matters because of my Foreign Office postings and of my continuing activities with Moral Re-Armament as a means of helping this cause. His reply was: 'But the two approaches should run together, shouldn't they?' and it was on that basis that I took the job. Thus began, unexpectedly, a further two years of highly interesting work on world development problems.

I had met Edward Heath only once before, when he was Prime Minister and I was escorting the Tunisian Foreign Minister on an official visit to Britain. Since then he had lost the prime ministership to the Labour Party in the 1974 election, and subsequently the leadership of the Conservative Party to Mrs Thatcher in 1975. I therefore met a slightly saddened man, conscious that he was no longer holding high office as the Queen's first minister and yet still immensely able. He gave the air of a rather lonely man, and yet a glance around his London home showed what a full life he was still leading. Photographs and mementoes from the world of sailing and the world of music showed how he excelled in both, while still playing a very active role in politics. The one question which my first conversation with him provoked was how much time and energy he was going to devote to Third World problems as compared with all his other interests. His past political record did not produce a clear answer to this question, for his priorities had been Britain's relations with Europe and Britain's own economic survival. I think it is probably true that, at the time of his acceptance of membership in the Brandt Commission, he himself may not have been clear on his future priorities and may have been subconsciously trying to fill a gap in his life. What I am sure about is that the deeper he got involved in Third World problems, the more his commitment grew; and it could be argued that in the end there would have been no Brandt Report without him.

It is said that Willy Brandt consulted a group of German psychologists on the optimum size of the Commission and they assured him that 18 was the maximum number to have a chance of achieving unanimity in discussing such matters. Brandt therefore settled on 18 commissioners, plus three ex officio members and a panel of eminent consultants on development matters. The Commission was a distinguished body including senior representatives from many walks of life – politicians, international civil servants, representatives from business, trade unions and the media; from rich countries and poor; from all faiths and none. Brandt was disappointed that the Soviet Union and China refused to be represented on the Commission, but he visited Moscow and Beijing to collect their ideas and to have consultations with them.

For such a varied group to reach unanimity after two years of discussion on a programme of action, including priorities, to advance world development and assist developing countries was no mean achievement, and it did not happen easily.

Fairly early in the Commission's work a dispute arose between two members, one from the rich world and one from the poor. It was a conflict of personalities as much as a disagreement over the agenda. The Commission's sessions were private, but after a meeting in Kuala Lumpur news of the dispute leaked to the media. At that point I had the clear thought that I should be ready to try to do something about this problem. The thought was wholly unexpected and I at first resisted it on the grounds that this issue went beyond my sphere as a research assistant. But when I talked to the private secretaries of the two statesmen involved, I found they shared my concern and were keen that I should do anything I could to help. I therefore sought separate appointments with the two commissioners and tried to explain how costly the dispute might prove in relation to the Commission's task if it were allowed to grow. My points were absorbed almost silently and I can only think that a Higher Wisdom must have given weight to my words, because from that day the atmosphere in the meetings began to improve. What I could not possibly have foreseen was the consequences of my small initiative in the following year.

The Commission was then moving towards the end of its labours and was meeting in Brussels to consider a first draft of its report. Unfortunately it turned out to be a very bad session with dissatisfaction and dissent being voiced all round the table. Finally Willy Brandt announced in despair that he could do no more and was departing for Germany, leaving the Deputy Chairman, L K Jha of India, in charge. On that unhappy afternoon the only thing on which all the members could agree was to hand over all the documentation to the two men who had been in dispute at Kuala Lumpur in the previous year and to promise to try to support whatever compromise text they could produce in two months' time. When I saw this plan take shape I thought gratefully of how the two men in question had risen above their differences and, as statesmen, had combined their talents for the completion of our work.

The final meeting of the Commission duly took place in the picturesque setting of Leeds Castle in Kent, arranged by Edward Heath, and there the new draft of the Report was unanimously agreed. When it was released publicly it made headlines around the world. It was translated into numerous languages and was hailed by Lord Carrington, the then British Foreign Secretary, who had not originally been a fan of the Brandt Commission, as 'the publishing success of the year'.

During the final frantic weeks of the Commission's work I found myself as one of an editorial group of five who had ultimate responsibility for producing the text to be considered at Leeds Castle. It was intensive, round-the-clock work with rigid deadlines, and once again I learned – at some cost to my own pride – how crucial the human factor can be in such a negotiation. One of our small group was – so it seemed to me – delaying our work by repeatedly demanding insertions or qualifications regarding the legitimate role of multinational companies. I felt that this point had already been underlined in the report and I fear I lost patience. I made sarcastic jokes about my colleague which amused the others in the group but certainly did not amuse him. That evening, before going to bed, the thought came to me: 'Today you made an enemy,' and I realised that I needed to apologise, both for my sarcasm and my impatience.

Next morning when I reached the office, my troublesome colleague was in the elevator. So I made my apologies as we mounted to the fifth floor. My colleague did not say much, but once again the atmosphere in our meeting changed perceptibly and we managed to meet our deadlines. But the bonus for me was that the troublesome colleague became a permanent friend.

The ultimate success of the Brandt Commission depended on the response of governments, especially Western governments, to what we proposed, and here the outcome was disappointing. A world summit conference was called at Cancún in Mexico to consider the report. It was attended by Ronald Reagan, Margaret Thatcher and many other world leaders: but despite the publicity, very few governmental commitments were forthcoming and it seemed to us on the Commission that an opportunity was lost.

However that may be, it is certainly true that the Brandt Commission moved the whole question of development and the bridging of the North-South gap higher up the agenda for action, and many things happened in the ensuing decade that would not have happened but for its work. For me personally it had been a stimulating experience which had a pleasant postcript. At the final dinner at Leeds Castle, Willy Brandt's secretary had quietly handed me a sealed envelope. In it I found a brief note of thanks for my 'special services' to the Commission. What made it specially pleasing was the fact that the letter was signed not by Willy Brandt, but by the two men who had been involved in the dispute at Kuala Lumpur.

So here we are 20 years on, and the development issue,

the Rich-Poor gap, is still very much with us. Many vastly different attempts have been made to tackle it in the last two decades. UN negotiations have continued almost non-stop in many different forums. The major nations in the G8 group have got it high on their agenda at most meetings. The World Bank and the IMF have come up with numerous proposals. Bob Geldof's initiatives seized many headlines. Special interest groups and intelligently-led NGOs have redoubled their efforts. Debt relief campaigns like Jubilee 2000 have made at least some impact on the seats of power. And now, more controversially, we have militant anti-capitalist campaigns and violent demonstrations in major cities, professing to be helping the Third World but doing much harm to innocent individuals and private concerns caught in the cross-fire with security forces.

It can confidently be asserted that never before have so many people been involved, directly and indirectly, in schemes for alleviating world suffering, and never before has so much publicity been generated – thanks to television and the ubiquitous media – on such phenomena.

So what can be concluded from the fact that all these efforts together have hardly dented the basic problem? Clearly, these Rich-Poor differences go much too deep for painless cures or facile panaceas. They seem to be endemic in the human condition. Must we then accept a completely pessimistic view of the universe? Are some problems insoluble and getting worse?

The positive efforts referred to above suggest that all is not yet lost. The younger generation, although so blasé about conventional politics and other democratic responsibilities, do care about this issue. Balancing the hedonistic pictures of yuppies in their wine bars or at drug raves are other pictures of young people sweating it out on projects in remote developing countries. And no less striking is the generosity of people of all ages to emergency appeals after earthquakes and floods.

Human nature has more potential in it than is suggested by Machiavelli or Hobbes. Short bursts of altruistic behaviour do happen. What is more difficult is to get sustained commitments to long-term remedial efforts. The NIMBY instinct ('not in my back-yard') is also strong in all of us.

Moreover, the overall problem is not created by failures in only one privileged part of the world. I recall an American diplomat telling me of a covert investigation carried out by the US Government in one Latin American country which had revealed unmistakably that more funds were leaving that country for private banks in Florida and Switzerland than the total amounts of foreign aid going into the country from the USA and other international donors.

Perhaps we get nearer the truth by reminding ourselves of an old piece of English doggerel:

> 'There is so much good in the worst of us,
> And so much bad in the best of us,
> That it ill behoves any one of us
> To throw mud at the rest of us.'

What is certain is that much more than charitable appeals or international resolutions would be needed to make an impact on such problems: and also more than any amount of technology. We would need a new kind of moral commitment world-wide if we are going to cure corruption in the developing countries (and in rich countries) no less than to crack the selfishness of the Western world.

I still have in mind the anguished appeal of a young Buddhist monk when I was visiting Cambodia on an aid-giving mission in the 1980s. He was one of the relatively few survivors of Pol Pot's savage assaults on all religious institutions. We were sitting in a clearing in the jungle while UN trucks from Thailand trundled past carrying in drinking water and other forms of aid. The young monk said: 'Yes, we need material aid very much. But, oh please, give us back our sense of right and wrong.'

13

Faith in Diplomacy

Some time after I had retired from the Diplomatic Service came the memorable day, 15th November 1979, when Mrs Thatcher stunned the House of Commons, and the whole nation, by revealing that Anthony Blunt had been under suspicion of espionage for several years, and had been repeatedly reprieved (retaining his post in Buckingham Palace), but had finally been arrested. On that afternoon I happened to be working with Edward Heath in his London home, and I said to him that I felt as if I were somehow personally involved in this astonishing sequence of events. I then told him in detail how the years during which Blunt had been under investigation had happened to coincide with the years during which I was being regularly cross-questioned by Foreign Office security officials as a possible security risk because of my links with MRA. Edward Heath remained silent and then offered only one comment. He said, 'These were years of which our country can never be proud.'

From an early stage in my career I was aware of suspicion in certain official quarters about my association with Moral Re-Armament. I would not suggest for a moment that this was dominant among my colleagues. On the contrary, I had the happiest of working relations over many years with the vast majority of them. And it is to me a striking fact that I was never once criticised by any of my own bosses for my links with MRA. Nor did any of them suggest that this reduced my usefulness to them. Indeed I happen to know that several of them wrote privately to the relevant quarters in London to defend me against attack or innuendo. And I had the good fortune to serve under a number of the most outstanding members of the Diplomatic Service in my time.

However, from the early 1950s onwards I was periodically made aware of this pall of suspicion. I remember an occasion at the time when I was one of the leaders of the British team working on the problems of disarmament and the then head of the Foreign Office issued an instruction that I should be 'moved to less sensitive work'. I had never met the person in question and so the background to this proposal must have been written reports from unnamed sources. The instant reaction from my immediate bosses and also the Minister in charge of Disarmament (Anthony Nutting) was that this was ridiculous and that I 'could not be spared': and the issue was quietly dropped. It was galling, however, to think that I was under suspicion for taking a stand on moral principles at a time when the Foreign Office, reeling from the aftermath of the Maclean and Burgess scandal, was having to circulate memoranda warning members of the Service that there was a disturbing increase in security problems arising from excessive drinking and sexual irregularities. To my mind MRA – far from being regarded as a cause of suspicion – should have been welcomed for its contribution to strengthening public and private morality. Somehow, however, the idea had been sown that I – and MRA – were security risks. Conceivably someone theorised that my loyalty to the principle of absolute honesty might result in my revealing, or indeed proclaiming from the roof-tops, secrets about British foreign policy. It seemed to me almost infantile to interpret absolute honesty as being a licence to blurt out confidential information to all and sundry. In reality, the principles of MRA should to my mind have been recognised as a bulwark to national security.

The suspicions which were evident in my case came to a head after the incident in Iran which I have recounted already. I was then invited, indeed urged, to resign from the Service. Faced with this threat to my career I resorted to the right of every member of the Service in such a situation to put his case before the Foreign Secretary personally. I was therefore given an appointment with the Earl of Home (Sir Alec Douglas-Home), who was then Foreign Secretary, in the presence of one of my accusers.

It turned out to be a surprising occasion. I took the opportunity to express in full to Lord Home the basis of my personal faith and the nature of my associations with MRA. I reaffirmed my wish to continue to work in the Diplomatic Service and my readiness to be bound by all its regulations. In reply he confined himself, as I recall, to saying that I must recognise that MRA was controversial in certain circles. Even one of his own relatives, he said, would 'turn puce' at the mention of Frank Buchman. I therefore must be cautious. I said that, as one Scot to another, I had no difficulty in giving him such an assurance. The interview then finished by his saying: 'I think you will probably be in the Foreign Office longer than I shall.'

The handling of security problems in democracies is admittedly a difficult matter, and especially in organisations such as the Foreign Office: and I do not think either the Foreign Office or the Security Services would claim to have a perfect record in this sphere. Nor do I pretend to any omniscience either. For example, I knew both Donald Maclean and Guy Burgess quite well. Maclean was a First Secretary in the Washington Embassy when I was there.

He was obviously thought of as a 'high flyer' by his superiors and was being groomed for promotion. I knew him as a personable individual, son of a respected Cabinet Minister of the Thirties, and I never suspected that he was then making regular trips to New York to hand over hundreds of secret documents to his Russian contact. So I was blind. Of course, his Washington years were a sober period for him. It was after his transfer to Cairo that, presumably because of inner tensions, he became involved in drunken brawls and scandals which even resulted in damage to American Embassy property. But it is worrying to think that even after these episodes, he was transferred to another key post in the Foreign Office.

Guy Burgess was another type altogether. Despite his bohemian charm and intellectual agility, he was obviously an erratic individual and I can recall tense moments in Paris, where we were both attending a UN conference, when his briefcase went missing and was only found hours later in one of the seediest Parisian night clubs. Like many others, I was astonished when it was proposed later that he should be transferred to Washington and was accepted by the Ambassador there. Official blindness to the risks which Burgess posed proved costly for the whole British nation. There is no doubt that moral weakness played a part in the extraordinary duplicity of men like Maclean, Burgess and Philby. The Foreign Office was obviously attaching more attention to skills than to character in its handling of them. Yet Jules Cambon, one of the great figures of French diplomacy, maintained that 'there is nothing so powerful as the honest word of a decent man'.

In my own case I have no hesitation in saying that my links with MRA strengthened my character. This is not a boast; it is just the result of honest reflection on my own nature, strong points and weak points, over the last 80 years! I started off with the genes of a normal Scot, and I had the benefit of a good family upbringing. But my contact with MRA brought an extra dimension into my life. In particular, it was this contact which introduced me to the concept of a daily time of moral and spiritual meditation which changed my life-style and has remained my regular habit early every morning for the past 68 years. For me this is essentially a Christian practice, but the concept is one shared by all the great faiths.

One can indulge in endless metaphysical and psychological speculation on the process by which God communicates with men. What I am sure about is that this practice of listening, supplemented by reading from the Bible and other books, and by prayers of supplication, has shaped me into what I am. The so-called 'quiet time' has helped in many ways:

It added discipline to my life.

It has provided orientation, illumination, correction and direction.

It has been a never-failing rudder.

It enables me to check up on my own performance.

It has freed me from the rat-race.

It helps me to reach out to others.

It often results in my doing things I would not otherwise do.

It also, from time to time, yields wholly unexpected insights of great value.

It would be hard to deny the value of such benefits in a period of social confusion and psychological disruption such as we live in today.

That a loving God, personified for me in Jesus Christ, should wish to communicate with men and women on a regular basis seems almost a self-evident truth. I recall what Abraham Lincoln said: 'I am satisfied that when the Almighty wants me to do or not to do any particular thing, he finds a way of letting me know it.' As the prophet

Isaiah said, long before Abraham Lincoln: 'Thine ears shall hear a word behind thee saying, "This is the way, walk ye in it, when ye turn to the right hand, and when ye turn to the left."' And in our own day, Dag Hammarskjöld put it: 'The best and most wonderful thing that can happen to you in life is that you should be silent and let God work and speak.' Winston Churchill too, not only complained of 'the black dog' of depression that occasionally afflicted him, but spoke of the influence of 'some guiding hand' at various points in his career. If we are often not conscious of God's communications, may this not be due to the fact that we do not give enough time to letting him speak?

I do not claim any gifts as a seer, nor do I hear voices in any literal sense: but what I know is that by following this practice, I have repeatedly found that there is, after all, a way out of an impasse; that when I seemed to be alone, I found an ally standing with me; that when I seemed to be facing a solid stone wall, a door would appear. Looking back on my career I feel that one of the most rewarding and interesting episodes was my assignment to Yugoslavia. Yet, as will have been clear from earlier chapters, my arrival there was not particularly auspicious: nor was it a step up the career ladder. But what followed strengthened my personal belief that, if one is faithful to one's vision – whether or not that be popular – one gets used in unexpected ways.

This turned out to be true at many points in my own experience: for example, the urge to inject something new into the preparations for the crucial Special Session of the General Assembly on the world oil crisis; or to admit a personal fault, as happened more than once during my work with the Brandt Commission. The experience of which I speak, known to countless thousands all through history, is not just an intellectual one, and certainly not the result of abstract logical deduction. Perhaps it could be better described as 'a spirit of discernment'. Many would call it conscience; but to me it is something more than that. It has been well said that conscience tells you the difference between right and wrong, but this experience tells you which of several courses, all potentially good, is the right one.

It is also certainly not just like a switch to be turned on and off by whimsy. It presupposes a readiness to believe and obey the thoughts that come, or what the down-to-earth mediaeval mystic Brother Lawrence called 'the practice of the presence of God'. It also turns out to be a confirmation of the biblical truth that 'He that doeth his will shall know of the doctrine, whether it be of God'. (St John, chapter 7, verse 17, AV).

The thought of a daily time of meditation early in the morning, when one's mind and spirit are freshest, is not necessarily the most congenial idea to those whose style of living and source of happiness depend on 'partying' till the small hours: but it is a normative experience open to absolutely everyone. And to those who hesitate through fear of becoming victims of hallucinations or 'evil spirits', the simplest of checks is available: do the thoughts square with absolute moral standards, for example with the principles in the Sermon on the Mount?

All these experiences have been confirmations to me of the truth of the Bible story I related at the start of this book, of the man who performed a well-nigh impossible task demanded by his master, and who explained his achievement very simply by saying: 'I, being in the way, the Lord led me.'

At one point in my career I found to my surprise that, in a breakdown of my financial emoluments supplied from the Foreign Office, I was listed as a 'non-alcoholic' and £100 had been deducted from my pay. This seemed all the more bizarre because it happened just after we had been inspected in Burma by a joint team of Foreign Office and Treasury experts who had told my wife and myself that we were spending too much on official entertaining and that we could not expect to be recompensed in toto from public funds. The reason for our large-scale expenses was in fact due to the extraordinary position in which the entire British commercial community found itself, following the coup d'état by the Burmese military who, in a paroxysm of xenophobia, were threatening to confiscate all assets of foreigners. As I have related, rings were even being pulled from the fingers of foreign women on the pretext that the sapphires and rubies in them must be Burmese property. My job as Commercial Counsellor in the Embassy was to assist the British commercial community in every way I could, some of whom were on the verge of nervous breakdowns. This was the reason for our unusually high entertaining bills. We tried to do our best, but it would have been an odd kind of help if we had just encouraged them to drown their sorrows in alcohol – as many were tempted to do.

In fact, my wife and I got many letters of appreciation for our efforts. At our departure from Burma, the most senior British commercial representative in Rangoon, Brigadier George Todd, Chairman of Burma Mines, wrote to thank us for our 'consideration and hospitality' and continued: 'You leave in the knowledge that you have earned the deepest respect of all the commercial world of Rangoon. I, in common with the others, am sincerely grateful ... you will be sorely missed.'

It is distasteful to seem to be blowing one's own trumpet, but sometimes it is necessary to balance the record in view of wildly inaccurate tales that are occasionally disseminated, and in view of the fact that, as already explained, we were leaving Burma with a warning of 'no more promotion' in our ears and with £100 less in our pockets for being 'non-alcoholic'.

Sometimes I used to take refuge in the saying of Thoreau: 'If a man does not keep pace with his companions, perhaps it is because he hears a different drummer. Let him step to the music he hears, however measured and far away.'

The problem of what to do when one finds oneself in disagreement with one's own government's policy is one that faces every diplomat. The careerist will doubtless suppress his doubts and do what he is told. The more conscientious will ponder, realising that as long as he (or she) is a member of the Service he has an inside track for bringing pressure for change to bear on his own government. After all, a considerable part of a diplomat's time is spent on informing his government about the exact circumstances prevailing in his area – often on the other side of the world. He can fill in the gaps in their knowledge and try to correct distorted perspectives or dangerous miscalculations made at his home base. In the end, of course, he has to decide whether to carry out his instructions or offer to resign. I felt very conscious of the fact that I might at some stage find myself in that predicament, and I knew which way I would go.

Fortunately, I never found myself faced with that dire choice. If I had been responsible, for example, for carrying out Middle East policy at the time of the Suez Crisis in 1956, I can well believe that I might have had to resign. And there were times when I knew I was courting unpopularity in Whitehall by offering views which ran counter to the current trend of policy in London. I also did my best wherever I was to encourage my staff to think and act constructively and keep the longer-term in view rather than to give way to nationalistic or racial reactions. What I could never have done, given my commitment to live responsibly by moral principles, would have been to allow internal divergences of view to lead me into betraying my government or my country – although that seemed to be the half-expressed fear behind much of the cross-questioning to which I was being subjected.

Even after my interview with Lord Home I found on my next return to London that the cloud of suspicion against me had not been entirely dispelled. I was again called in for a security briefing. There was nothing abnormal about that, but the flat-footed way in which I was questioned by a non-Foreign Office official showed me that, at least in some quarters, I was still deemed to be 'a risk'.

The theory seemed to be that any association with an organisation such as MRA which promoted a programme of moral standards might somehow result in a conflict of loyalties or in British official secrets being noised abroad. In this situation I felt I had no option but to raise the matter with the head of the Foreign Office. I said that, in spite of my interview with Lord Home and the assurances I had given him, I was still clearly an object of suspicion and unless this stopped I would consider raising the issue with my Member of Parliament. Fortunately, the head of the Foreign Office at that stage, Paul Gore-Booth, was an eminently fair-minded individual. He asked me to take no action and promised that he would personally supervise a review of all the matters on my personal files. Some weeks later I was called to his office and he indicated clearly to me that, in light of what he had found, he felt that a review had been justified. He said: 'However, I can assure you that your file is now perfectly clean.' From that time onwards I detected a different tone in all my dealings with the Personnel Division.

I would only add that the events of which I write in this chapter happened over 30 years ago. Most of the people closely involved are dead and all have long since retired.

And I can well believe that the attitude of the authorities concerned is very different today and that the prejudices and suspicion to which I have referred have been dispelled.

14

New Dimensions of Statecraft
– where are we going?

There are endless definitions of what exactly diplomacy is
– from the comic and satirical to the most erudite. One of
the more amusing ones takes the form of a riddle. Why is
a diplomat like a duck? Answer: Because they both look
smooth on top; but underneath they are both paddling like
hell.

Diplomacy is, of course, a very ancient profession going
back to biblical times. It is also peculiar in that it has two
very differing traditions attaching to it: the high and noble,
and the low and disreputable. According to the first, a
diplomatic envoy is the personal representative of a
monarch and arrives bearing gifts. This tradition survives
in such customs as 'kissing hands' with the Queen before
an ambassador goes abroad to present his ornate 'letters of
credence' to another head of state.

Actually, the kissing of hands now amounts to a pleasant 20-minute chat with the Queen in Buckingham Palace
in which the ambassador's wife also takes part. But I have
one giddy recollection of being confronted with this very
noble face of diplomacy. In our Embassy in Tunis we were
entertaining a party which included a lady belonging to
one of the oldest aristocratic families in England who happened to be visiting North Africa. Moreover, she herself

was then being dubbed by society magazines as one of the two most beautiful women in Britain. As we received our guests, I was taken aback when the vision of loveliness before me curtsied elegantly. I suppose I blushed, but then I quickly recollected that our guest moved in royal circles, as had her husband's family for centuries, and that she was curtseying not to me as a humble member of the Mackenzie clan but to the ambassador as the personal representative of the Queen in that country at that time.

According to the other tradition, a diplomat may be charming but is fundamentally insincere, guilty of double-dealing and prone to spying. One classical definition, capable of many interpretations, was offered by a 17th century Englishman, Sir Henry Wotton: 'An ambassador is an honest man sent to lie abroad for the good of his country.'

Much evidence could be produced to support both of these traditions but I think it is unfortunate that some of our best thriller writers, even John le Carré, fail to draw a clear enough distinction between the sphere of orthodox diplomacy and the cloak-and-dagger activities of the clandestine agencies which commonly masquerade around the world under sets of initials and numbers.

What cannot be denied, however, is that even orthodox diplomacy has become a much more dangerous profession nowadays. I have had five personal friends, all senior diplomats, who have been assassinated: two British colleagues killed by the IRA in Dublin and The Hague; a German friend killed inside the German Embassy in Stockholm by the Baader-Meinhof gang; a Yugoslav diplomat gunned down in Munich, almost certainly by another Yugoslav; and a South Korean friend killed by North Koreans in Rangoon, along with half the South Korean Cabinet, in the middle of a state visit to Burma.

Today, however, professional diplomacy is being

attacked and belittled on new grounds. It is suggested that the revolution in communications has rendered diplomats superfluous and out-of-date. The international media and the Internet and email can together do much more swiftly all that diplomats used to do very laboriously; and government ministers and officials from capitals can fly out to foreign trouble-spots within a few hours. Why then maintain expensive embassies manned by expensive diplomats all round the world?

It will be clear from the earlier chapters of this book that I do not accept this theory. It is true that diplomats have less power today than in previous centuries. To talk of an 'envoy plenipotentiary' has ceased to have meaning. The diplomat's role has changed, but it has not disappeared. Nor can experts flown out from capitals at a moment's notice replace the man-on-the-spot who has systematically built up valuable contacts, and even friendships, in the other country concerned. My own experiences in Burma, Yugoslavia, the United Nations and other places convince me of that.

When one thinks of the extraordinary expansion of multilateral diplomacy, or conference-diplomacy, since the Second World War, and the proliferation of UN Specialised Agencies, added to the traditional tasks of bilateral diplomacy, one realises that a diplomat's field of activity, and therefore of influence, has never been so great. He can find himself dealing with the consequences of an air crash, the building of a dam, commercial contracts, atomic energy, the law of the sea, Third World development, and scores of other issues.

It is also a fact that much of the physical hardship associated with overseas service in previous centuries has now been overcome. The aeroplane, the air-conditioner, the mobile phone and email have transformed life abroad for diplomats and their families. Contemporary conditions of service are not likely to drive a diplomat's wife ever again to threaten to write her memoirs under a title such as *Lend Me Your Plastic Flowers*. Today women occupy an increasing number of posts in the higher echelons of the Diplomatic Service, and rightly so; but the recent best-seller *Daughters of Britannia* by Katie Hickman (Harper Collins 1999) contains vivid reminders of the valiant contributions of women to diplomatic life in past centuries as well.

Unquestionably, diplomacy has become far more technological since my time. Some people would now say it is a science rather than an art. Yet however technical it is, it remains true that while you can plan a new world on paper, you have to build it out of people. As Her Majesty the Queen observed as far back as 1983 in her Christmas broadcast: 'Electronics cannot create comradeship. Computers cannot generate compassion. Satellites cannot transmit tolerance.'

I remember, while working with the Brandt Commission, having the impression that I had read over a hundred economic treatises and dissertations all ending with the same six words. Having analysed the problems and made recommendations for solving them, they concluded:

'Therefore X or Y is the answer *provided the necessary political will exists.*' The implication was that the experts had thus fulfilled their obligations; but in fact that is where the real battle begins between theory and practice. How do you create the political will for peaceful change? How do you deal with the obstacles of entrenched selfishness or inflamed nationalism?

The Brandt report did recognise this issue. It said: 'No matter how enlightened the plans for the economic and social betterment of people's conditions, they will achieve little unless in parallel the battle is fought at the same time in both North and South to liberate people from outworn ideas, from the grip of narrowly conceived national interests and from the passions and prejudices inherited from the past. A new international economic order will need men and women with a new mentality and outlook to make it work.'

Immanuel Kant was facing this reality when he said, in words often quoted by Isaiah Berlin: 'Out of timber so crooked as that from which man is made, nothing entirely straight can be built.' This is doubtless true, but the consequence is that professional diplomacy, whether working through the UN or in other ways, needs to pay more attention than has often been the case to the irreducible human factor in all social and economic issues. That is why I feel that morally and spiritually-minded bodies, like MRA and many others, and professional bodies like the Foreign Office, should regard each other as allies, if not partners. It would be ridiculous to suggest that unofficial bodies could somehow replace the efforts of professional diplomats: but would it not also be fair to say that bodies like the Foreign Office would be ill-advised to spurn help that may be forthcoming from unofficial bodies with special knowledge or special contacts in different parts of the world?

To one who has pursued a lifelong interest in 'the ethical implications of democracy', it is encouraging to notice a broadening recognition of these forgotten factors that should lie behind, and underpin, effective diplomacy. Despite many worrying trends and gloomy prognostications at the start of the new millennium, these developments seem to me to be causes for hope.

One such development was the publication in 1994 of a volume entitled *Religion – the Missing Dimension of Statecraft* by the Washington think-tank, Center for Strategic and International Studies (OUP, edited by Douglas Johnston and Cynthia Sampson). This ground-breaking work argues that most Western thinking on international affairs has suffered from a blinkered outlook dating back to the anti-religious prejudices of the Enlightenment movement of the 18th century. As a result of these secularist assumptions, Johnston says that 'we inadequately appreciate the transformational possibilities that exist when the parties involved in a dispute can be appealed to on the basis of shared spiritual convictions or values.'

The book recognises that religion is, sadly, all too often a cause of, or a contributory factor to, contemporary conflicts in many parts of the world; but in its case-studies it shows how religion, rightly used, can contribute positively to reconciliations and political settlements. It recognises too the difference between religion as a focus for identity (in which context it can readily be a divisive factor), and religion as an energising and purifying force in individual lives. 'Reconciliation born of spiritual conviction,' it says, 'can play a critical role by inspiring conflicting parties to move beyond the normal human reaction of responding in kind, of returning violence for violence.' The book acknowledges that far greater research is needed in these fields, but its case-studies on the resolving of recent disputes in Europe, Africa, Asia and Central America are genuinely encouraging.

A second positive development, closely associated with the foregoing, is the growing attention being paid to what the American scholar and diplomat, Joseph Montville, has called 'Track Two Diplomacy'. Track Two diplomacy refers directly to the contributions that can be made, and are being made, by unofficial agencies when official diplomatic efforts have ground to a halt. By their very nature such initiatives are informal and often pass unnoticed. The Oslo Process of the early 1990s, whereby the Middle East peace negotiations were restarted, is the best-known example of this, even though it has sadly not yet resulted in solid agreements. Track Two diplomacy is what Chancellor Adenauer of Germany was referring to when he said that Moral Re-Armament had played 'an unseen but effective part' in relation to various European agreements after the Second World War, and the specific example of French-German relations is also spelled out in the CSIS study. It shows clearly how individuals or unofficial agencies with a moral and spiritual input can be catalysts which start up positive reactions. They can help to break deadlocks and so free the hands of the professionals to get on with the technical tasks.

In recent years Moral Re-Armament, renamed Initiatives of Change in 2001, has also been developing new techniques for working in this field. In addition to its major world conferences at Caux and elsewhere, it has promoted a number of targeted programmes which are producing interesting results through Track Two diplomacy methods. One, entitled Agenda for Reconciliation, selects particular conflict situations such as the Horn of Africa and pursues in depth – through sessions at Caux and visits to the area – the search for the deeper experiences of restitution and forgiveness between individuals and groups which can lead eventually to political reconciliation. A second programme, entitled Foundations for Freedom, has focussed on the problems of Eastern Europe since the collapse of Communism. Through intensive short courses in many European countries it has encouraged young graduates to face the need for a moral infrastructure on which to build the fledgling new democratic régimes. British government funds have assisted these efforts. A similar programme called the Caux Scholars Program has for the last ten years been giving selected young graduates from around the world an imaginative in-depth training in the real ethical issues lying behind the now popular academic themes of 'conflict resolution'.

Meanwhile, yet another programme, called Hope in the Cities, has been developed in the USA, but increasingly also in Britain, to deal with the alarming breakdown of social and ethnic cooperation in so many Western conurbations. All these programmes carry forward the basic insights contained in the concept of Track Two diplomacy.

A third hopeful sign was the note struck by Kofi Annan in his Millennium Report to the United Nations. In language unusual in an intergovernmental report, the Secretary-General called on the member states to 'form coalitions for change, often with partners well beyond the precincts of officialdom'. This is in line with the course of action I have been advocating in this book and, if followed, could open the door to greater use of Track Two diplomacy.

The Secretary-General's dictum is also a reminder of how much the world has changed since the drafting of the Charter in San Francisco. In 1945 nation-states were regarded as the only actors on the international scene. They were viewed like shiny billiard balls – although of differing sizes – which were constantly in motion, and the main challenge in international affairs was to prevent them from colliding too violently. Since then the sovereign powers of nation-states have been whittled down drastically from two sides: on the one hand by the technological revolution which has propelled us all into an interdependent world – and by the related expansion in the power of multinational companies; and on the other by the rise of well-armed and highly mobile extremist groups, bound by ethnic, religious or other grievances, who can pose threats even to the most solidly established nation-states. The catastrophic events in New York and Washington on 11th September 2001 were dramatic reminders of these new dimensions of terrorism and of the difficulty of handling them by conventional methods.

The whole doctrine of national sovereignty therefore needs to be re-examined. Which attributes are essential to sovereign survival and which can be surrendered? Some attitudes of sovereignty may be inevitably cancelled out by changing world conditions; and others may be voluntarily surrendered – as inside the European Union. But voluntary surrenders are proving extremely controversial, even when done on a small regional scale, and there is so far little sign of a willingness to make such surrenders on a global scale – as in the United Nations.

Thus the nation-state may still be the only building block for the construction of a global society, but new balances of power will have to be sensitively worked out. The new thinking advocated by Kofi Annan will need time to grow; and there will also have to be a readiness to sacrifice short-term to long-term interests before agreements will be possible. The much-talked-of 'globalisation of opportunities' will have to be matched by a 'globalisation of responsibilities', as has been emphasised by Cornelio Sommaruga, formerly head of the International Red Cross and now president of the Swiss Foundation for Moral Re-Armament, as well as being a member of Kofi Annan's panel for reforming the United Nations security system.

No one can pretend that such a fundamental alteration from current practice will be an easy task, especially as the powerful tendencies moving us towards 'one world' are often counter-balanced by fierce demands for local independence from smaller units – as inside former Yugoslavia – and even of xenophobia inside old established states. At times it seems as if humanity today shares the predicament of the poet who felt himself to be 'wandering between two worlds, one dead, the other powerless to be born'. What is certain is that a high level of moral enlightenment, not just technical skill, is going to be needed to see us through these difficulties.

A fourth hopeful factor, also at work within the UN, is the research being done on the concept of 'preventive diplomacy', or 'preventive action' in the latest parlance. This was started by Boutros Boutros-Ghali and has been continued under Kofi Annan. Preventive diplomacy refers to the fact that many international conflicts might have been avoided, or at least alleviated, if attention had been paid to them sooner, before the grievances and bitterness exploded into a dispute that needed to be handled by the Security Council. This is true of problems like the break-up of Yugoslavia, which eventually threatened to desta-bilise the whole of the Balkans, but which had their roots in divisive tendencies which had been visible in the area for at least a decade. Similar rumblings of discontent must have been audible to those with ears to hear before large-scale massacres erupted in Rwanda and Burundi and other African trouble-spots.

As long as the Cold War raged, it was difficult to handle many recognisable problems, especially in Eastern Europe, simply because any signs of outside intervention, or even of concern, were liable to precipitate a clash between the Great Powers. Inaction over known problems was often an unhappy by-product of the Cold War. After 1989 this com-plication was removed but, of course, it still remains diffi-cult to get overworked governments to focus on problems that can be deferred, or swept under the carpet for a little longer – especially if financial outlays are involved.

However, this is precisely the area where unofficial bod-ies or the UN Secretariat can play a part, at least in ensur-ing that such warning signs are not ignored. Moreover, the drafters of the UN Charter did foresee this problem and deliberately gave the Secretary-General himself the power 'to bring to the attention of the Security Council any mat-ter which in his opinion may threaten the maintenance of international peace and security' (Article 99). This gives a

Secretary-General considerable scope for preventive action, provided he has the necessary back-up in the Secretariat's research departments, and provided he has the courage to risk the displeasure of the member-states involved.

This will always remain a sensitive area. The expenditure of money is almost inevitably involved and this poses special problems for democracies and for international organisations. It is also the point at which international and domestic concerns often collide. How can a national government advocate controversial and possibly expensive action in a hypothetical crisis when a general election may be in the offing at home? In the last resort, therefore, action in the sphere of preventive diplomacy will depend on the state of public opinion, whether enlightened or inward-looking, and on the quality of political leadership available. Public opinion polls, which are supposed to be tools for the promotion of genuine democracy, can also stifle creative initiatives. No speedy solutions to such problems may be forthcoming, but it is at least encouraging that the potential of preventive diplomacy is coming under urgent scrutiny.

There is no denying the complexity of formulating foreign policy in present-day conditions. Outside pressures, not necessarily from foreign sources, bear in on the Foreign Office all the time. Not so long ago a friend in the Foreign Office said to me, 'You'll never believe how many foreign policy issues are now decided in the Treasury and not here.'

Money is a constant constraint on Foreign Office initiatives. This applies specially in anything to do with military action or peace enforcement. There is often talk of possible European military action without the Americans, but a US Army officer cut through much of this rhetoric by saying: 'But where's your HLC?'

'What,' I asked, 'is HLC?'

'Heavy Lift Capacity,' he said, and went on to argue that the most advanced military equipment and the best trained troops count for virtually nothing without the giant transport planes and patrolling aircraft carriers needed to get them rapidly to areas of conflict. Up till now Europe has quietly relied on the Americans to make us truly operational.

Moreover, pressures on the Foreign Office can take many other forms. It was alleged that in the Western military action in Kosovo in 1999 lawyers, not generals, often had the last word. This was apparently true even in the selecting of bombing targets, so great was the sensitivity of public opinion over the legality of allied action and over the consequences of possible mistakes. Further, it was evident, at least in the USA, that the emotive publicity campaign about 'body bags' was a major determinant of American policy.

Given these considerations, and the unprecedented capacity of the media to embarrass governments, fairly or unfairly, the prospects for rapid and decisive action by the United Nations – dependent as it is on the approval of member governments – are admittedly not great.

Occasionally, however, as I have just been arguing, developments occur that give one hope. Another such development was Prime Minister Tony Blair's speech to the Economic Club of Chicago in April 1999, in the middle of the Kosovan conflict. This may have been, I venture to suggest, one of the seminal speeches of the last part of the 20th century, like Winston Churchill's earlier speech at Fulton, Missouri.

Blair was outlining what he called 'the beginnings of a new doctrine of international community' and he called for far-reaching changes in international trade, finance and environmental policies, plus a more constructive and inclusive attitude to Russia and reforms in the United Nations, NATO, IMF and the World Bank. He also proposed a Marshall Plan for the Balkans and declared squarely that 'the most pressing foreign policy that we face is to identify the circumstances in which we should get actively involved in other people's conflicts.' He went on to list five tests by which to make decisions on this delicate issue: 'Are we sure of our case? Have we exhausted all the options? Are there military operations that we can sensibly and prudently take? Are we prepared for the long term? And finally, do we have national interests involved?' Blair was speaking in 1999, and obviously this formulation requires much further thought and refinement in the light of subsequent events. But for those hoping to see the development of a truly international community in the 21st century, this speech offers a good rallying point.

Amendments to the UN Charter are long overdue. The 1945 version has served the world well for over 50 years but conditions have changed so radically in the interim that updating is obviously necessary. This will not be easy, as any amendments are subject to the veto provision, ie they must be supported by all five Permanent Members. In particular, it seems to me that three changes are needed. First, the membership of the Security Council needs to reflect more accurately the distribution of power at the present day, and that must mean a higher role for Germany and Japan and greater representation of Asia and Latin America. Secondly, the restrictive power of Article 2.7 regarding matters within domestic jurisdiction needs to be curtailed – as I have already explained and as Tony Blair has confirmed – in order to give the organisation greater capacity to safeguard human rights wherever they are endangered. And thirdly, Article 43, under which member countries were supposed to make armed forces available to the Security Council 'on call', and which has been a dead letter for 55 years, needs to be re-examined in order to improve the UN's peacekeeping capacity.

But of course, the full flowering of the UN's potential needs much more than that. The ad hoc amendment of the Charter, even if attainable, is one thing: the revitalisation of the moral infrastructure of the organisation is quite another. The expert body appointed by the Secretary-General in 1999, headed by Lakhdar al-Brahimi of Algeria, to review the organisation's peace-making and peace-keeping operations concluded that the technical reforms needed would require nothing less than a 'doctrinal shift' in the United Nations – a changed mind-set. This recalls the experience of William Wilberforce who set out to abolish the slave trade but who found himself drawn willy-nilly into a wider struggle to achieve 'a reform in manners' of the whole British nation. Kofi Annan was pointing in the same direction when he called, in his Millennium Report, for the member-states and their leaders to make nothing less than 'a moral recommitment' to the purposes of the Charter.

This opens up philosophical issues that are not often referred to in the day-to-day operations of the organisation. It may be ill-advised for political leaders to use slogans about 'Back to Basics' or to emphasise 'the ethical dimension of foreign policy' unless they are ready to follow through on the implications of such statements for themselves and their parties. But the slogans themselves have important truth in them. Even Lord Keynes, the most eminent of economists, predicted that the day would come when 'the economic problem will take the back seat where it belongs ... and the arena of heart and head will be occupied where it belongs, or reoccupied by our real problems, the problems of life and human relations, of creation, and of behaviour and religion.'

I have indicated that my own philosophical roots go

back to Immanuel Kant and his Categorical Imperative: 'Act only on that maxim through which you can at the same time will that it should become universal law.' But I am happy that I can also draw on support from Adam Smith, better known as the champion of free enterprise. Smith was professor of moral philosophy in my Alma Mater, Glasgow University, for years before he wrote his economic masterpiece on *The Wealth of Nations*. His insights on human nature are no less interesting than his rationale of free enterprise, and his doctrine of the 'Impartial Spectator' as a referee in judging the fairness of economic initiatives belongs more to Kant's world than to John Hobbes or John Stuart Mills. The Impartial Spectator inside each of us, or 'the demi-god within the breast', says Smith, 'is there to speak both for itself and for others ... In the race for wealth, if injustice is done, the Impartial Spectator changes sides.' In other words, if we get behind Smith's eighteenth century language, there are such things as innate moral standards and we are not guided solely by gain or greed. There is 'the man within us', or conscience, that we need to listen to, for he is 'the Vice Regent of the Deity'. And in the final analysis, according to Adam Smith, we need to 'co-operate with the Deity and advance, as far as is in our power, the plan of Providence.'

With such a perspective Frank Buchman would have found himself in full sympathy and so, I suspect, would such spiritual giants of our time as Mahatma Gandhi, the Dalai Lama, Pope Jean Paul II and Archbishop Desmond Tutu. Whatever doctrinal differences may exist between them, they would all endorse this moral philosophy as a guide for the United Nations and humanity. They would agree that the UN needs a moral and spiritual dynamic to help it deal with such basic human weaknesses as hatred and cynicism, corruption and egotism, and to enable it to tap into higher sources of wisdom. And of course, in such a spiritual odyssey there is another categorical imperative that applies: 'Everyone must start with themselves.'

I have tried in these pages to explain how this process has been going on in my own life. I think this book has been worth writing not because of its eloquence but because it does deal with important things. In Plato's words, in *The Republic*: 'Our discussion has been about no ordinary matter, but on the right way to conduct our lives.' I do not for one instant claim to have arrived at the goal. But I have found it an absorbing journey so far. I hope I have also conveyed at least something of its fascination and that the story will assist others facing challenges of discernment.

Index